THE COMPLETE
BACK GARDEN
BIRDWATCHER

THE COMPLETE
BACK GARDEN
BIRDWATCHER

DOMINIC COUZENS   Photography by **STEVE YOUNG**

NEW HOLLAND PUBLISHERS

First published in 2005 by New Holland Publishers (UK) Ltd
London • Cape Town • Sydney • Auckland

www.newhollandpublishers.com

Garfield House, 86–88 Edgware Road, London W2 2EA,
United Kingdom

80 McKenzie Street, Cape Town 8001, South Africa

14 Aquatic Drive, Frenchs Forest, NSW 2086, Australia

218 Lake Road, Northcote, Auckland, New Zealand

ISBN 1 84330 959 9

Publishing Manager: Jo Hemmings
Project Editor: Gareth Jones
Editor: Ben Hoare
Designer: Adam Morris
Index: Angie Hipkin
Production: Joan Woodroffe

Reproduction by Modern Age Repro Co., Hong Kong
Printed and bound in Malaysia by Times Offset (M) Sdn Bhd

PREVIOUS: *Nuthatch.*

Contents

Introduction *6*

Introduction

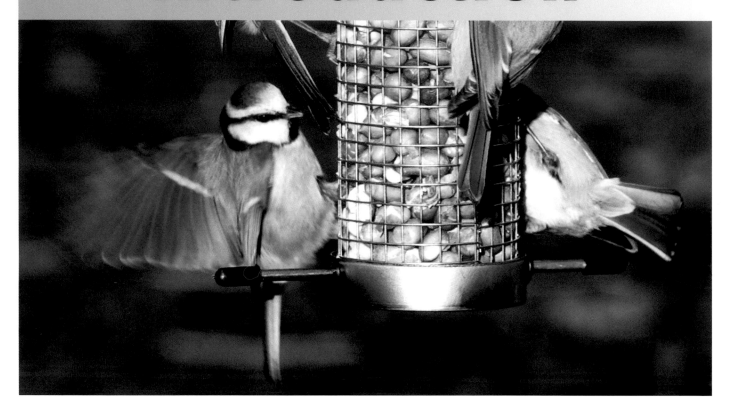

Books on garden birds are as numerous as Blue Tits on a well-stocked bird feeder, so why produce another one? Well, the fact is that most garden bird books tell you how to identify birds and how to attract them to the garden, as this one does in part, but they devote much less space to understanding garden birds, or else ignore the subject completely. This book helps to fill that gap. It is very much written from a birdwatcher's point of view, rather than for a person dedicated to wild bird husbandry. It helps you to look at the 'customer' on the bird table, and then beyond.

There are six chapters, each concerned with a different aspect of birds and gardens. The first is a catalogue of birds you might see, full of hints about how to identify them; its aim is to be reasonably complete and it features some more unusual garden visitors. It is followed by a chapter that includes a summary of the characteristics and behaviour of the more important species, describing events that you have a reasonable chance of witnessing for yourself. The third chapter describes the bird songs and calls you might hear in your garden, and the fourth provides a month-by-month calendar of the lives of your feathered neighbours. The fifth chapter delves into the needs of garden birds and suggests, where possible, how you can help to fulfil them. Finally, the sixth chapter includes a discussion about problematical or controversial issues to do with birds and gardens.

Throughout the text there are a few special projects that should, if you decide to undertake them, help you to look at your birds closely, and perhaps get even more satisfaction from watching them.

ABOVE : *Blue Tits at a feeder.*
OPPOSITE: *Juvenile Great Spotted Woodpecker.*

Chapter 1

Identifying Birds

This chapter introduces you to the company of birds that might visit your garden. There are quite a lot of them and, if you are fairly new to birdwatching, you might like to browse this section as you would a catalogue, getting to know the names, appearances and specifications of each one. Once you have got beyond the 'catalogue' stage, there is a definite technique for learning to identify birds well, and that's to look at them objectively. This is the fast-track method, which will help details to stick in the mind. If you can, describe a bird thoroughly and systematically to yourself while you are still watching it (I'm assuming you will be using binoculars). Start at the head and finish at the tail. Note the shape of bill, tail and head, as well as scrutinizing and judging the colour. If you wish to assess a bird's size, do so in reference to a nearby bird that you already know. A bird's apparent size is highly variable – for example, birds look larger when back-lit – so it is best not to use this feature too much.

ABOVE : *Jay.*
OPPOSITE: *Waxwing.*

Mallard

This is a bird that comes in a variety of shapes and sizes. But whatever the colour and pattern, if you have a visit from a duck in your garden, it will invariably be a Mallard. Any other duck in the garden would almost be a miracle!

The typical drake Mallard has an iridescent bottle-green head and a cute curly tuft on its tail (this must be something of an embarrassment to it). The female is brown and speckled, with quite a stern look upon her face. Many of the more wacky

Grey Heron

You are not going to be visited by any other tall, grey, long-legged birds, so the Grey Heron should not present any identification challenge. A Grey Heron in flight is as distinctive as one on land. A number of birds have big, broad wings that are flapped slowly, including the Buzzard, swans, geese and large gulls, but none of these trail their long legs behind them.

ABOVE LEFT: *Adult (right) and juvenile (left) Grey Heron.* **ABOVE RIGHT:** *A female Mallard, showing its dull brown plumage.* **BELOW:** *Adult Grey Heron in flight.*

Tip

You can sometimes tell the age of your visiting heron by looking at its head. Adult herons have a white crown, with a black stripe below that runs into a plume. If the individual in question has a grey crown and no black stripe, it was hatched last spring.

ABOVE: *A group of 'Yuk Ducks' showing variation in the Mallard's plumage.* **BOTTOM LEFT:** *Mallards often 'up-end' to get food from the bed of the pond. Here a pair are working in unison: male (left) and female (right).* **BOTTOM RIGHT:** *Buzzard in flight. Note that the tail is as long as the wings are broad from front to back.*

versions of Mallards, such as those illustrated here, arise from what we might term as errors of copulatory judgment on behalf of one parent or the other. A scientist would term it inherent genetic variation; birdwatchers call them 'yuk ducks'.

Tip

Drake Mallards adopt a sort of 'drag' plumage in late summer (July–September), in which they look like females. However, you can still identify them by their yellow bills.

Buzzard

Only the more countrified gardens will have visits from Buzzards, and these visitors will probably only fly over, without touching down.

The Buzzard is a large bird – far larger than any of the other birds of prey you will see over your garden. It is best identified by its short, broad tail, which is often held fanned out. In level flight, it alternates a burst of stiff flaps with glides. When it is soaring – gaining altitude by flying in circles – it holds its wings up at a slight angle.

Tip

In a flying Buzzard, the tail is about the same length as the width of the wing (that is, the width across the wing, not the wingspan).

Sparrowhawk

Nowadays, the Sparrowhawk is the predatory bird you are most likely to see in the garden. Many individuals habitually terrorize birds at feeding stations, treating your bird table like a fast-food outlet.

On most of its visits you will have little time to observe a Sparrowhawk: the business is usually over very quickly. All you will see is a grey (male) or brown (female) shape, slightly larger than a pigeon, accelerating towards the feeder or slinking away, depending on how quickly its presence has come to your attention. You are as likely to hear the commotion from other birds as to see the hunter itself.

If you are ever fortunate enough to see a Sparrowhawk perched, you will always recognize it by the bars across its chest (Kestrels have spotty stripes down their chests). Males are blue-grey above and have a distinct orangey wash to the underparts; females lack any orange colouration, and are cold brown above and white below. Sparrowhawks have yellow eyes and a slightly staring, crazed expression that would not look out of place in a horror movie. Kestrels, on the other hand, have darker eyes and a slightly gentler mien.

> **Tip**
>
> Female Sparrowhawks are noticeably larger than males weighing as much as one-third more. Apart from the plumage differences already mentioned, see if you can get a grasp of this distinction.

TOP RIGHT: *Male (left), female (right).* **RIGHT:** *A female Sparrowhawk watches the comings and goings of prey from a concealed perch.*

Kestrel

It is probably safe to say that not many gardens receive regular visits from Kestrels. A small number of individuals use Sparrowhawk-like tactics to ambush the birds on your feeder, but the truth is that Kestrels are not very good at catching birds and therefore don't try it very often. A lightning strike on feeding birds is likely to be carried out by a Sparrowhawk.

Kestrels do occur in both suburban and urban areas, however, and, if your garden is close to some wasteland or open country, you might be lucky enough to see them over your airspace. As likely as not they will be hovering – that is, flying on the spot – and scanning the grass below for small mammals.

It should be said that birdwatchers of many years' standing may still find it difficult to separate Kestrel and Sparrowhawk. The main reason for this is undoubtedly their similar size, and perhaps the fact that, unless the Kestrel is hunting, views of both species are usually rather brief. So brace yourself for the fact that you will not be able to identify every small bird of prey that you see.

However, with practice, the two species are distinguishable. In flight silhouette, the Sparrowhawk has short, broad and blunt wings. You can sometimes make out the 'fingers', or primary flight feathers, at the end of the wings. In contrast, the Kestrel has longer and much more pointed wings. This remains the safest way to tell the pair apart. Unless, of course, the bird is hovering, in which case it is definitely a Kestrel. Sparrowhawks just don't hover, ever.

The Sparrowhawk is a compact, purposeful bird of prey that moves along with a distinctive flight style: a series of 4–5 rapid flaps of the wings followed by a long glide, then more flaps, and so on. The Kestrel is a much more lightweight bird with a more 'flappy' flight. In level flight, it alternates a lot of flaps with brief glides, and it is much less purposeful and powerful-looking than a Sparrowhawk.

Tip

Take the outer part of a Kestrel or Sparrowhawk's wing to be the 'hand', and the inner part to be the 'arm'. The Kestrel has a longer, narrower 'hand' than a Sparrowhawk, while a Sparrowhawk has a broader 'arm' than a Kestrel.

ABOVE: *Sparrowhawk (left) – blunt-tipped wings, with 'fingers', and a squared-off tail. Kestrel (right) – pointed wings and a rounded tail.* **BELOW:** *Male Kestrel.*

Pheasant

This gamebird (a bird often shot for eating) is likely to be seen in and around gardens only in country-side areas. It lives on the ground and flies only when it has to. If you have a Pheasant in a suburban garden, it is lost!

The male Pheasant's shape is distinctive, although the colour may vary. The female is a small brown version of the male, but you won't get anything else shaped like this turning up between your garden's four walls.

Tip

You can tell the origin of your male Pheasant easily enough. If it has a white ring around its neck, its ancestors came from China. If it lacks a neck ring, its forebears came from the Caucasus Mountains in Central Asia.

ABOVE RIGHT: *When calling to advertise its presence on territory, the male Pheasant flaps its wings rapidly at the same time as it makes its 'coughing' sounds.* BELOW: *A female Pheasant searching for seeds in the snow.*

Black-headed Gull

Gulls can be a touchy subject among birdwatchers. If birders do not, like most people, have an inherent dislike of gulls, then they find them horrendously difficult to identify and therefore ignore them. However, if you force yourself to start looking at gulls, you might just find yourself thawing slightly towards them. You'll be well on the way to gull demystification.

gulls are perched, look for the red or orange bill and legs, which are unique to this species, and the dusky spot behind the eye. If they are flying, note that their wings are elegant and pointed, and that there is a triangular patch of white on the front edge of the wing.

Tip

It is relatively easy to age a Black-headed Gull because this species matures quickly. Any bird with brown on its wings and a black band on the end of its tail will be a first-winter individual; these are seen between September and February. Any bird without both of these features will be an adult.

The fast-track route to bird identification described in the introduction to this chapter is particularly important when it comes to gulls. You really need a strong empirical image of the bird in your head to have any hope of identifying it. For example, if you observe the general colour of the plumage but forget to look at the leg colour, you are stuck.

The elegant Black-headed Gull is by far the commonest gull found inland, so it is also the one that is most often seen flying over gardens. The main problem with identifying it is that it lacks the expected black head, both in breeding plumage (February–July) and in non-breeding plumage (August–January). Don't ask why: nobody seems to know. Instead, at least during the breeding season, it has a distinctive smart brown head.

Unfortunately, the non-breeding season is when you are most likely to see this bird in the vicinity of your garden, usually in flocks or small groups. During this time you need to look out for other features. If the

ABOVE: *Adult Black-headed Gull in winter. Note the red bill and legs, plus the smudge behind the eye.*
OPPOSITE BOTTOM RIGHT: *Black-headed Gull in flight. Take note of the diagnostic white 'triangle' of white on the leading edge of its wings.* BELOW: *First Winter Black-headed Gulls retain brown on their wings, and have red or orange bills and legs.*

Herring Gull

It is mostly those people who live in coastal areas that will see these large, noisy gulls on a regular basis. Indeed, the birds may well be all too familiar. They are loud and brash, confident and, at times, almost menacing. They hold court in the vicinity of fast-food restaurants and may well rob you of your fish and chips. They hang around on roofs in seaside towns and seem to do very little all day. Actually, they fit rather well into Britain's yob culture.

The adult birds are easy enough to recognize, with their white head, body and tail, cold grey back and wings, and black-and-white wing-tips. They have flesh-coloured legs and their yellow bill has an orange spot at the tip (the young gulls tap this 'button' to stimulate the adults into regurgitating food for them). Herring Gulls have a distinctly frowning expression, which, when combined with their pale eyes, gives them a rather fierce appearance.

The various immature plumage stages of Herring Gulls are very difficult to get to grips with. Suffice it to say that, over the four years a Herring Gull takes to mature, it becomes progressively whiter and less brown.

ABOVE: *Note the black-and-white neck-collar and washed-out plumage of the Collared Dove.* **BOTTOM LEFT:** *The confusing plumages of Herring Gulls. Flying: adult (right) and first winter (left). Standing: adult (top); first winter (bottom right); second winter (left, below adult).*

Collared Dove

Pigeons and doves belong to the same family, and the terms 'pigeon' and 'dove' actually overlap. The white 'doves' released on ceremonial occasions to promote peace and harmony, for example, are actually Feral Pigeons, while the Woodpigeon used to be known as the Ring Dove. But most birdwatchers regard doves as smaller and slimmer than pigeons, and the Collared Dove fits this perception well. It is definitely the Weight Watchers' darling of the family, being much the slimmest of the group. It is quite streamlined, with long wings and tail.

Collared Doves have a curious plumage, which is a sort of creamy-brown, anaemic colour that varies a little according to the prevailing lighting conditions. Fortunately, they have a diagnostic white-bordered black ring around the sides and back of the neck.

Tip

With practice, you can pick this species out by its manner of flight, even from a great distance. In contrast to our other pigeons, which flap up and down in straightforward fashion, the Collared Dove has a distinct flicking action, with intermittent fast, deeper wingbeats and brief glides. It also has much more swept-back wings.

Woodpigeon

The much-misunderstood Woodpigeon must be familiar to almost everybody. It is the large grey pigeon with the prominent white patch on the side of its neck, and the one with the yellow eyes that give it a perpetually astonished gaze. With the pink wash to the breast, lichen-green patch above the white on its neck, and bold wing markings, it is actually a fairly attractive bird, but its abundance has the effect of decreasing our appreciation.

By virtue of flocking with identical members of its own kind, all looking the same, the Woodpigeon is easily separated from the Feral Pigeon, flocks of which tend to include birds in a dolly-mixture of different colours.

Two features on the Woodpigeon's wing distinguish it from other pigeons at all times. In flight, each wing has a white middle bar separating the inner wing from the outer wing, and this bar curves slightly inwards. These white bands are roughly

where the engines would be on an aeroplane. The other feature is on the folded wing. If you look closely, you'll see that the main flight feathers, the primaries, are edged with white. Not particularly important, you might think, but very useful if you cannot see the bird's head properly.

ABOVE RIGHT: A Woodpigeon in flight. Take note of the diagnostic white band across the wing. **BELOW:** *Adult Woodpigeon with the smart white mark on its neck and lemon-yellow eyes.* **BELOW RIGHT:** *The juvenile Woodpigeon lacks the signature white splodge on the neck.*

Tip

Juvenile Woodpigeons entirely lack the signature white patch on the neck and also have a dark eye – so watch out for those wing features. Juveniles are most common in summer but can, in fact, be seen in any month of the year.

Stock Dove

Some gardens receive visits from a smaller pigeon called the Stock Dove. Despite lacking all of the Woodpigeon's key features, it is still very hard to distinguish. In fact, it is often the Stock Dove's shape that stands out at first, especially when it is perched or standing: it is much more compact, without the 'beer gut' of a Woodpigeon and with a much shorter tail. The Woodpigeon sometimes looks as though its tail has been stuck on later, but the well-proportioned Stock Dove never gives this impression.

The Stock Dove has black – not yellow – eyes and entirely lacks any white on the neck, although it does have iridescent green on the sides (and very attractive this is, too). It is also a darker, neater, smokier grey than its relative. But those wings are again important: the primary feathers entirely lack the white edges of a Woodpigeon, being entirely black. The greyish inner wing is adorned with a couple of short rows of neat, button-shaped black spots. In flight, the Stock Dove has a decidedly grey-bordered-with-black look, which, when you get your eye in, enables you to pick it out relatively easily.

ABOVE: *The Stock Dove is an uncommon visitor to gardens.* **LEFT:** *A pair of Stock Doves. Notice their black eyes and complete lack of white on the neck or wing.* **OPPOSITE:** *A group of Feral Pigeons.*

Tip

The fast, flickering flight of the Stock Dove resembles the style of the Collared Dove, but it has a shorter tail and blunt-looking wings.

Feral Pigeon

If you are wondering what a 'Feral Pigeon' might be, it's the name given to those pigeons you see on urban streets and in town parks, the ones that display and copulate shamelessly on the ground while you are trying to feed them bread. They inhabit Trafalgar Square, St Mark's Square in Venice and many other places besides squares. They often spend a lot of time sitting on roofs.

Originally, the Feral Pigeon was a 'proper' species just like the Woodpigeon, with all the individuals looking the same and living in wild places. Known as the Rock Dove, it mainly frequented cliffs and mountains. Many thousands of Rock Doves were then brought into domestication. People started cross-breeding and otherwise interfering with the birds' genes, producing all kinds of varieties with different shapes, colours and characteristics. These included fat, edible ones, entirely white ones such as Fantail Pigeons, fast ones (racing pigeons) and reliable ones (carrier pigeons).

Many of these pigeons had productive domestic careers, but others, especially those kept for their flying abilities, occasionally went missing. Instead of disappearing into the wild, they found that towns and cities offered the chance of an easy life. They remained close to people and fed on city waste, especially grain. Thus the abundant, highly variable and streetwise Feral Pigeon was born.

This brief history explains one of the key features of the Feral Pigeon: the variability of its plumage. The average flock very rarely, if ever, contains a lot of individuals looking the same. There will be many different patterns in each group and perhaps pink, black, white and grey birds all consorting together. Apart from this, it is actually very difficult to pin down the identification points that clinch a Feral Pigeon. Most individuals have red eyes, which helps.

Tip

In flight, Feral Pigeons are slimmer than Woodpigeons and have faster wingbeats. One particularly useful characteristic visible on most birds is that the underside of the wing is whitish, which can give a sort of twinkling effect. None of the other pigeons or doves are predominantly white under the wing.

Birds as Individuals

It is usually impossible to identify birds down to the individual level – the species level is hard enough! But, with Feral Pigeons, it is often perfectly feasible, especially if you are going to break the habit of a lifetime and actually look at them closely.

Studies have shown that in urban and suburban areas Feral Pigeons live in small groups of around 10–20 birds that have a consistent membership. If food is always available, the individuals in these groups may not travel more than a couple of kilometres in their lifetimes, which is remarkable considering the navigational feats of racing pigeons. They may be longer-standing neighbours than most of your human ones.

If a Feral Pigeon flock regularly uses your garden, you could make a note of some individual features, or even sketch them. You can then see which bird is mated with which, which is the flock's dominant bird, which sits where on your roof, which comes down to the bird table and when. In a small way, it will be possible to follow the soap opera of their lives.

Ring-necked Parakeet

In recent years, some gardens in the London area and elsewhere have begun to receive visits from parakeets. They are not native birds, of course, but actually originated in India. They were brought to Britain as cage birds in the 1960s and it is assumed that a number escaped, although one cannot rule out the possibility that a number might have been set free deliberately ('Rodney, either that parrot goes or I do…'). They have been at large ever since, and, incredibly, they have some-how managed to cope with our climate. No doubt they have been helped by garden birdwatchers who put out suitable foods for them.

You won't have any trouble identifying a parakeet because it has bright green plumage, a hooked bill, fast flight and a long tail. However, you should bear in mind that a lot of species of parrots are kept in captivity (there are more than 300 species worldwide) and they are liable to escape from time to time. Cockatiels and budgeri-gars are quite often seen in the wild in Britain, leaving behind an empty cage and a tearful child.

Both sexes of Ring-necked Parakeet have a black line separating their head from the rest of the body. The male, in addition, has an attractive rosy-red patch on his nape.

Tawny Owl

A good many neighbourhoods have owls, which, of course, can normally be heard only at night (see page 110) and are seldom seen. 99 percent of these visitors are Tawny Owls because the garden habitat simply does not suit the other species. In Ireland, however, the common owl is the Long-eared Owl, since 'Tawnies' do not occur there.

The Tawny Owl is quite a large species with a round face and dark eyes. It has a pleasing brown plumage with an intricate pattern that blends in wonderfully well with tree bark. By day, it tends to rest in a hole or in a thick part of the foliage well up in a tall tree, where it may be almost impossible to see.

You probably won't glimpse a Tawny Owl unless you have quite a large garden or a neighbourhood with trees at least as tall as two-storey houses. And then you must go outside and take your chances at night. Another possibility is to watch a quiet road lit with street-lights, since Tawny Owls often catch food on roads. In summer, when Tawny Owls are feeding young, they are slightly easier to see; they may even be moderately active in the daytime. The youngsters are cute and fluffy, with a gormless expression

OPPOSITE TOP: *Ring-necked Parakeets are regular visitors to bird tables only in a few parts of Britain, especially the London area.* OPPOSITE BOTTOM: *The lack of a rosy ring around this bird's neck indicates that it's a female.* ABOVE: *Fluffy and cute they might look, but these young Tawny Owls will grow up to be killers.* LEFT: *A Tawny Owl at roost. Note its dark eyes and the similarity of its plumage to the tree bark.*

Tip

Note how the Tawny Owl flies on a straight course with quite stiff, rapid wingbeats. The flight of other owls is quite different. The Long-eared Owl has a much more wavering, hesitant flight, often stopping almost to hover. For the Little Owl, see page 22.

Little Owl

This is the only other owl that is likely to be seen in gardens, and then only in those that adjoin farmland and fields bordered by willows and other more substantial trees. If you can see an open field with fence posts from your back window, you are in with a chance.

The Little Owl is about the size of a large thrush, although in dim conditions, when it is silhouetted, it often looks much bigger. It has quite long legs and a short tail. In comparison with the Tawny Owl, it is usually paler brown (exactly the colour of willow bark), with yellow not black eyes, prominent white eyebrows and heavily white-spotted plumage.

Where it occurs, the Little Owl is always much easier to see than the Tawny. It is frequently active in the daytime, flying from tree to tree or post to post, and sometimes perching freely in the open. Oddly, though, this species hardly ever feeds during the day: perhaps it just can't sleep.

Should you see a Little Owl fly for any distance, its manner of flight will be very distinctive. It flies on a real up-and-down course – a bounding flight more typically seen in smaller birds such as finches. But beware of two other birds with similar flight styles that live in similar places and are not much different in size: these are Mistle Thrush and Green Woodpecker.

Tip

Try to look at the back of a Little Owl's head. You will see broad, pale markings similar to those on the front. These 'eyes in the back of its head' are intended to deter predators from catching Little Owls, but both Tawny Owls and Sparrowhawks sometimes do.

ABOVE: *Even in the middle of the day Little Owls are often alert and awake.* **LEFT:** *The yellow eyes and white 'eyebrows' of the Little Owl give it a fierce look.*

Tip

In contrast to Swallows and House Martins, Swifts quite often close up their forked tail to make it into a spike.

LEFT: *The classic scythe-like shape of a flying Swift.* **BELOW TOP:** *House Martins have much shorter tails than Swifts or Swallows with a shallower fork. They also have white underparts and a diagnostic white rump.* **BELOW BOTTOM:** *Swallows have longer tails than Swifts, and are pale below. Note how the join between wing and body is broader than that of the Swift.*

Swift

The first thing to say about the Swift is that it is the definitive high summer bird. You will only see it over the garden during the cricket season, from the beginning of May to the end of August. The Swift never perches or settles on the ground, so the garden birdwatcher will only ever see one flying. It builds a nest in a crevice near the top of a tall building such as a church tower, well out of sight, and on most summer days it will simply ride the skies above rooftop height.

Two other garden birds are primarily aerial: the Swallow and House Martin. In common with the Swift, they snatch all their insect food in mid-air. But the Swallow often perches on wires and aerials to sing, and both it and the House Martin sometimes come to the ground to collect mud for their nests. The House Martin regularly clings to the side of its mud structure below the eaves of a house. The Swift does none of these things.

The illustrations show the distinctive shapes of all three species. In particular, notice the point at which the wing joins the body. In a Swift the connection is narrow, whereas in both Swallow and House Martin it is much broader. Plumage-wise, the Swift is easiest to identify because it is simply black all over, save for a little patch of white on the throat like a child's bib.

Green Woodpecker

Given a reasonable view, you are not going to have trouble identifying a Green Woodpecker: it is our only woodpecker of such a colour, but telling males apart from females is a good challenge. The difference comes down merely to a marking on the cheek. The male's 'moustache' is crimson-centred with a black border; the female's is simply black, with no crimson. It is a small difference and hard to see because sometimes you have to wait for the bird to turn its head before you can see the male's red patch glinting in the light.

All woodpeckers, including this one, fly with a 'bounding' or 'undulating' flight pattern, taking them up and down as they move forwards. They fly with intermittent bursts of wingbeats, perhaps three or four at a time. The wingbeats take them upwards, their momentum allows them to level out, and then they drop down slowly, only for the next set of wingbeats to carry them upwards again.

ABOVE RIGHT: *The Green Woodpecker, along with the other woodpeckers, has a distinctive bounding flight action.* **BELOW:** *Both sexes of Green Woodpecker have brilliant red on the head, but it's the moustache that counts – red in the male (left), black in the female (right).* **BELOW RIGHT:** *This is the only woodpecker that is normally seen on the ground.*

Tip

If you see a woodpecker flying low to the ground, it's a Green Woodpecker. If it is nearer treetop height, it's a Great Spotted Woodpecker (or, if you are extremely lucky, a Lesser Spotted Woodpecker).

Great Spotted Woodpecker

This is by far the commonest woodpecker found in gardens and it is the only one that will visit bird tables and feeders regularly. It is mainly black and white, and is about the size of a Starling. Nevertheless, size is a very subjective quality. Just because a woodpecker might look slightly smaller than you might expect, that does not make it a Lesser Spotted Woodpecker. Birds often look different according to the lighting conditions and how far they are from the observer. The only way to be sure you are lucky enough to have a

visit from a Lesser Spotted Woodpecker is to scrutinize its plumage closely (see next section).

The Great Spotted Woodpecker is mostly black and white, and on its wing is a large white 'slab of paint'. All adults have a scarlet red patch under their tail. Males and females are very similar, but the male alone has a little spot of red on his nape. As in the Green Woodpecker's moustache, this can be tricky to see, especially if the light is not very good.

In the summer, roughly between June and September, you might well have a visit from a juvenile woodpecker. Juveniles of both sexes have a bright red cap, so they are quite easy to separate from older birds.

> **Tip**
>
> It is possible to sex young Great Spotted Woodpeckers. Males have a greater extent of red on the cap.

ABOVE: *Juvenile Great Spotted Woodpeckers have a lot of red on the cap.* **RIGHT:** *A young female Great Spotted Woodpecker showing black on the nape and a few red spots on the crown.*

Lesser Spotted Woodpecker

These days the smaller of our two black-and-white woodpeckers is becoming a rare bird, and only a few privileged gardens receive visits from this secretive sprite. Having said that, if you are in the south of England or the Midlands and you are not completely subsumed by the great suburban sprawl, it is a bird you should look out for.

You will never become truly familiar with the Lesser Spotted Woodpecker, even if it does live in your neighbourhood. For this is a shy, quiet species, which, unlike other woodpeckers, often moves from place to place without ceremony, and which tends to remain high and unseen in the topmost twigs of large deciduous trees. It can occur in an area and not be seen for long periods of time – even years; in a period of four years I have seen it only once in my garden, although it undoubtedly must breed nearby. The ultimate prize, a visit by a Lesser Spotted Woodpecker to a bird table or feeder, is an extremely unusual event indeed.

This woodpecker is smaller than the Great Spotted Woodpecker; in fact, it is not much larger than a sparrow. It's a woodpecker in miniature, creeping

rather than jerking about in the branches and having a petite mien that is difficult to define. Put simply, the Lesser Spotted Woodpecker just does not look or act like its larger relative.

Getting down to the empirical nitty-gritty, the Lesser Spotted Woodpecker can be instantly recognized by the parallel white stripes across its back, like the rungs of a ladder. It also has a few black streaks down the side of the breast. It lacks the red under the tail of a Great Spotted Woodpecker and also the larger bird's white 'blob of paint' on the back. Given a half-decent view, it is not especially difficult to identify.

In summary, 99.9 percent of the black-and-white woodpeckers that visit gardens, and especially feeding stations, are Great Spotted Woodpeckers. Therefore, never expect to see a Lesser, but simply hope for a welcome surprise.

Tip

In flight, the Lesser Spotted Woodpecker follows the usual undulating path of all woodpeckers, but often with higher peaks and lower troughs than the others. If a woodpecker seems to land unusually high in a tree, making for the small and thin branches of the canopy, it might be this species.

LEFT: *A male Lesser Spotted Woodpecker sports a red crown, so beware of confusion with the larger juvenile Great Spotted Woodpecker.*

LEFT: *The female Lesser Spotted Woodpecker lacks any red on the crown, just a white forehead and black on the nape.* **BELOW:** *A rare sight indeed – the streaky-crowned, slightly dusky juvenile.*

Swallow

The celebrated Swallow is a summer visitor to Britain's gardens, generally arriving in the first week of April and departing in September and October. It is common and widespread but is not keen on suburbs, so to have Swallows breeding nearby you will need to be in the countryside or in an area with open fields. However, during the migration seasons, which are roughly April–May and August–October, you may see small parties of Swallows flying over your house, well above rooftop height.

Identifying the Swallow sounds easy. Of all our aerial birds – a group that includes the House Martin and Swift – it has the longest, most forked tail. It is the only one with the combination of a pale belly and dark throat (red above a breast-band of dark blue), the only one with a reddish forehead, and the only one with nothing but blue on its upperside (see House Martin), and it has a longer silhouette, especially to the rear. It perches far more frequently on wires, aerials and fences than the House Martin; the Swift never perches.

This all sounds ridiculously easy, but for some reason it isn't. To tell Swallows, Swifts and House Martins from one another requires practice, especially since all these species spend a great deal of time flying, often quite fast and far away.

The diagram below shows how the three species fly in different ways and at different heights. The distinctions are not definitive but are a good rule of thumb. Two species are definitely 'sweepers', flying in wide arcs and straight lines: the Swift generally feeds well above the treetops, reaching altitudes of up to 1,000 metres (3,280 feet) or more; the Swallow sweeps fast and low over fields, dodging cows and other obstacles, rarely flying much above rooftop level, except during migration, as previously mentioned. Swallows, in particular, often seem to ply a beat over a field, flying over it back and forth, again and again. Both of these species have power in their flight and a sense of direction and purpose lacking in House Martins.

The House Martin flies in quite a different way. It usually catches its food at higher levels than the Swallow, but does so with a more fluttery, weak-looking flight than either the Swallow or the Swift. It glides far more than the former and its 'turning circle' is often quite sharp, so that its flight path describes a scribble in the sky, with many changes in direction. It seems to dither rather than having a plan – definitely not a Type A personality.

ABOVE LEFT: *A female Swallow (centre), with its relatively short tail, faces a choice between males. On the left, a high-quality male with a symmetrical tail; on the right, a less desirable male whose tail streamers are of different lengths (see page 81).* **LEFT:** *When looking for food, Swallows perform long sweeps low to the ground, while House Martins and Swifts fly higher. The Martins feed at moderate height, gliding, twisting and turning regularly; the Swift plies higher altitudes in long sweeps.*

Tip

It is possible to sex *and* age Swallows, especially when they are perched on wires. Males have longer tails than females, and adults have longer tails than juveniles.

House Martin

This member of the aerial bird community usually arrives not before the second week of April at the earliest – slightly later than the Swallow – but leaves our shores at a similar time to it – in September and October. In contrast to the Swallow, it breeds deep into the heart of suburbs and even cities, using the eaves of buildings for its nests. It is not reliant on fields; gardens and streets are fine. It is a colonial nester, although most gatherings contain only a handful of pairs.

The House Martin is very smart and clean in appearance, although its glories are not always easy to appreciate. The white on its breast is as perfect as the deepest, richest matt paint, the sort that adorns an immaculate wall in a TV commercial, soft lighting and all. Its upperparts are blue-black and they are, in painting parlance, distinctly glossy.

If you are starting out as a birdwatcher it won't be long before the subject of rumps comes up, and here's a perfect example. In contrast to the plain-backed Swallow, the House Martin has an impeccable white rump, providing sharp contrast to the back and to the tail.

Much the most compact of the aerial birds, the House Martin has a shape all of its own. Its tail is

relatively short and is only shallowly, although noticeably, forked. The wings look a little shorter and stubbier than those of a Swallow, and they tend to be held out rather than being swept back. House Martins do not often perch on wires, although they are quite capable of doing so.

Tip

Given a good view in strong light, it is possible to distinguish a juvenile House Martin from an adult. The breast looks dusky, not gleaming white, and the upperparts have not yet acquired their gloss. Juvenile House Martins are seen in Britain from July through to October.

ABOVE TOP: *If you see a House Martin coming down to ground to get mud for its nest, look for its distinctive white feathered legs.* **ABOVE:** *The white rump of the House Martin is its most distinctive feature.*

Pied Wagtail

The adjective 'pied' is used for quite a number of British birds, and is generally understood as meaning black-and-white in colour; in fact, the word means a mixture, as in a 'pie' that you eat. Hence our Pied Wagtail is a mixture of black-and-white.

Pied Wagtails are common throughout the country, although most households are more likely to see them in winter than in summer. You will almost certainly attract one at some time if you have a pond, and they also like closely cropped grass and tarmac – they love superstore car parks. Their greatest passion, however, is for roofs: they adore perching on them, running up and down the tiles and perching on the guttering. They also sit on aerials and overhead wires.

Perhaps the first thing you will notice about this bird is that it has a long tail that it constantly wags, hence the name. The second thing you might take in is that it runs or walks along the ground instead of hopping. The vast majority of small bird species hop, so this is a useful distinction. Notice how this bird runs along, stops, changes direction, quickly accelerates and slows down again. It might also leap into the air periodically to grab a passing insect. All this is very distinctive. In flight, Pied Wagtails have a very up-and-down, rollercoaster-like flight path, which may catch the eye.

So far, so good. But if you want to tell apart the different plumages of wagtails, things get much trickier. Find out how by tackling the Tip.

ABOVE: *This is a female Pied Wagtail, identifiable by its dark grey (not black) back.* **BELOW LEFT:** *In winter Pied Wagtails have a white throat and a 'black serviette' around the neck.*

Tip

Pied Wagtails are a good test of your identification skills because they have separate male, female and immature plumages, and distinct summer and winter plumages, too.

In summer, the male has a black back and crown and extensive black on its throat and chest; its white head markings are bold and clean. A female, meanwhile, has a dark grey, not black, nape and back; it has a smaller patch of black on its throat and breast, and the edges of its white face markings are more diffuse. In winter, the differences between males and females remain intact, but both sexes lose the black on their throats, leaving a well-defined black breast-band, like a bib.

Young Pied Wagtails a few months old are much paler and browner than adults. Their throat is bordered by narrow black stripes, and many have a distinct yellow wash to the face.

Grey Wagtail

Some birds have really inappropriate names, and the Grey Wagtail is one of them. It is guaranteed to confuse even quite seasoned birdwatchers. The fact is that the Pied Wagtail is greyer and duller than the Grey Wagtail and the Grey Wagtail is more obviously yellow than grey. (Oh yes, and there's a Yellow Wagtail, too, but it doesn't normally visit gardens, thankfully).

If your garden has a river nearby, or even running through it, you might well have these delightful birds as your neighbours all year round. If you have a pond, or even if your neighbour does, you are most likely to receive a visit in the winter, between October and March. In common with Pied Wagtails, Grey Wagtails like roofs and lawns, but they are more likely to perch on the branches of waterside trees.

It is very easy to tell a Grey from a Pied Wagtail once you have the name worked out, since it always shows at least some lemon-yellow on its

underparts – usually under the tail. Males in spring have completely yellow underparts and a smart black throat bordered by white. Females often show a little 'stubble' on the throat, but the yellow underneath is inevitably less intense.

In winter, Grey Wagtails are duller in colour, losing the black from their throats and much of the yellow from their breast and belly. And so, if you are in any doubt about your identification, just look at the legs. Grey Wagtails have pink legs, Pied Wagtails black.

The Grey Wagtail also has a longer tail than the Pied and, generally, a more elongated rear end. It is said to wag its rear more completely and to have more extreme undulating flight than the Pied Wagtail.

Tip

Young Grey Wagtails in their first winter of life have clean white throats and a hint of buff on the breast. Their bill has pink at the base, while that of the adult is all-black. In flight, all Grey Wagtails have a broad white wing-bar visible from both above and below.

Wren

Believe it or not, the Wren is one of our commonest birds, if not the most numerous of all. You wouldn't think so if you asked birdwatchers how often they had seen one – many rarely have a close view of the species from one year to the next. You can conclude from this that: a) there is probably a Wren or two in your own garden; and b) any Wrens will be very easy to overlook, even if they are present.

The Wren inhabits gardens all year round. It is difficult to see because it is very small – many people think that it is the smallest bird in Britain, but the Goldcrest (page 42) is actually slightly smaller – and because it spends most of its time hidden away. It creeps around like a mouse, often near the ground where the vegetation is thickest. It rarely comes out into the open, and then only for a moment.

The Wren is thus harder to see than to identify. Its tiny size and distinctive shape, with a plump body, short, cocked-up tail and long, slightly down-curved bill, make it unique. It also has a habit of sitting on a perch and curtseying slightly, bending its feet and also flicking its wings. In flight it does not undulate like other small birds, but bolts from one bush to another with whirring wings, often not more than a few centimetres above the ground.

Tip

Notice that the Wren has a pale eyebrow, also known in the trade as a supercilium. If you cannot see the Wren's rear end, this is a good feature to look out for.

OPPOSITE TOP: *Despite its name, the Grey Wagtail is more yellow than grey.* **OPPOSITE BOTTOM:** *Grey Wagtails are always found near water.* **BELOW:** *The Wren is a distinctive bird – if you can see it! Look for a tiny bird with a plump body and a short, usually cocked tail. Closer scrutiny reveals fine barred plumage and a distinctive white stripe over the eye (supercilium).*

Waxwing

The stunning Waxwing is a rare winter visitor to Britain, but when it turns up it quite often visits gardens. This species adores berries, and it is not unknown for birdwatchers to plant suitable berry-bearing plants in their garden with the specific intention of one day attracting a Waxwing, even if it finally comes 20 years later.

The first Waxwings arrive in October, although it is not until December that they usually arrive in force. If your garden is on the east coast of Scotland you might have a visit every few years, but in the south of England Waxwings only turn up when the berry crop in Scandinavia cannot support the Waxwing population, which might only happen every ten years or so. The last birds depart Britain for the north in March.

This gorgeous bird is unmistakable, but in flight it closely resembles a Starling, flying on a straight or slightly undulating course with whirring wings. In common with Starlings, Waxwings are sociable and appear in groups; some of these are small, some larger, with hundreds of birds.

Tip

Adult Waxwings have a broad yellow tail band and a complex wing pattern, with yellow and white tips to the primary feathers that make a line of 'ribs' along the edge of the wings. Birds that have hatched the previous breeding season (first-winters) have a narrow tail band and a white 'vertebral column', without any ribs.

ABOVE: *Waxwings love fruit of all kinds. They can eat over 600 berries in a single day!* **LEFT:** *This is an adult male Waxwing, with the 'ribs and vertebrae' on its wings and with the odd red, waxy tips to its secondary flight feathers.* **OPPOSITE TOP:** *Dunnocks are almost always seen creeping along the ground.* **OPPOSITE BOTTOM:** *Although looking superficially like a sparrow, the Dunnock has a distinctly slaty-grey wash to its head and upper breast.*

Dunnock

The Dunnock provides a good test for your identification skills and powers of observation. At first sight it is the archetypal small, brown, not very exciting bird. But since there are a lot of these sorts of species around, cracking the identification of the Dunnock will be a feather in your cap, and the start of demystifying the garden's more difficult birds.

A good look at a Dunnock will identify its key features. Working from the front backwards (as in the fast-track identification method, see page 8), you will see that it has a thin, dark bill. This immediately distinguishes the Dunnock from any thick-billed, seed-eating birds such as sparrows or finches, so it is a good start. The head, furthermore, soon reveals some neat ash-grey coloration, especially on the crown and the throat (which is unstreaked), but there is no distinctive pale eyebrow. The grey goes down on to the breast, and the underparts are streaked mainly towards the sides, or flanks. The legs are pink. On the upperside, the back is coffee-brown with thick black streaks, neatly arranged and flowing down like ruts. The wing is subtly patterned with a thin white wing-bar, but the tail is brown without any adornments at all.

Working through a bird like this is something of a chore and does not come naturally, but it is unfortunately essential. At least a Dunnock is likely to stay in sight for long enough to take most of it in.

In fact, you can also identify the Dunnock by its behaviour. It is a shy, skulking bird that is usually seen on the ground or on a fence. When feeding it has such a twitchy action that one would be forgiven for thinking that it was excessively nervous. The wings and tail are constantly flicked. It hops but also shuffles and creeps, often crouching down and covering its upper legs with its belly feathers, as if it were embarrassed by its thighs.

The Dunnock flies low and weakly, with a jerky action. It is usually a quick dash at low level into a bush.

Tip

Juvenile Dunnocks, which can be seen from June to August, have less grey on the head and underparts than the adults, and have closely packed, well-delineated dark stripes on the underparts.

Robin

This is not a bird likely to cause too many identification problems. Have you ever noticed, though, that the red breast is not actually red, but orange, and that it extends above the eyes onto the bird's forehead?

In late summer you will probably see juvenile Robins hopping around on your lawn. These lack the characteristic colour on the breast shown by adults, so they can be a little difficult to identify. In common with many adolescent humans, they are covered with spots, especially on the head, breast and back, but you should be able to pick them out by the species' usual plump-breasted shape, curtseying action and cocking of the tail. Some juvenile Robins have a tinge of ochre where the breast colour will later appear.

ABOVE: *The juvenile Robin (seen mainly June–August) is a messy plumaged, spotty bird with only traces of the orange breast.* **BELOW:** *Everyone knows the adult Robin.*

Blackbird

Almost every garden has Blackbirds. They are one of the very first species learned by people new to birdwatching; in fact, my two-year-old daughter is now an expert at recognizing them. They occur in gardens all year round and are often tame.

Male Blackbirds should cause no problems at all, with their black plumage and mustard-coloured orange bill. They strut across lawns with confident runs, stopping every so often to watch for movement in the grass. They can also hop with their feet together.

ABOVE: *Try not to confuse the speckled juvenile Blackbird (right) with a thrush (see pages 36–37).* LEFT: *The male Blackbird is jet-black with an orange bill and eye-ring.* BELOW: *The female Blackbird is dark brown, with a few streaks on the throat and breast. It lacks the colourful bill of the male.*

Females are less easy to identify with certainty. They are dark brown and have only a dirty yellow bill, lacking the rich glowing colour of the male. Some old bird books colour female Blackbirds all-brown, neglecting the fact that they are much paler on the throat and breast, with strong dark brown streaks. This latter feature could cause difficulty when separating the Blackbird and Song Thrush, although the streaks are definitely not spots and the lower belly is much darker, in contrast to the light background to the Song Thrush's spots.

Juvenile Blackbirds, seen in April–August, often cause problems because they really are spotty, and actually don't look very much like adult Blackbirds. The spots, though, are buff-coloured and they are small and very closely packed – quite different to the neat dark spots of a thrush. The juvenile Blackbird looks more like a giant juvenile Robin.

When alarmed, a Blackbird will fly straight for cover, only just above ground. On longer journeys, it has a jerky flight pattern with very full, slightly flickering wingbeats.

Tip

During the autumn and winter months (September–March), young male Blackbirds are quite easy to distinguish from adults. They have a dark (not orange-yellow) bill, black plumage that lacks the gloss of adult males, and slightly con-trasting brownish wings.

Song Thrush

If you see a thrush on your garden lawn, it will be one of two species, the Song Thrush or the Mistle Thrush. In fact, the Song Thrush is the more common of the pair, but Mistle Thrushes also find their way to some gardens and this may be confusing.

The Song Thrush is a small, neatly proportioned and compact thrush, distinctly smaller than a Blackbird and only slightly larger than a Starling. It always looks dapper and well turned out – a credit to the carefully tended gardens that it inhabits. It is a year-round resident, although it's usually much easier to see in late winter and spring, when the males sit on high perches and sing for hours on end.

Several clues on a feeding bird will point in the direction of Song Thrush. It will feed on the lawn within a few metres of cover; it will be richly coloured with a pleasing brown on the wings, back and tail; and its spots will be quite neatly arranged, almost in lines, so that the breast looks typically immaculate.

Look at the spots carefully and take in their exact shape. You will see that they are not round, in fact, but arrow-shaped, with the sharp end at the top. They point upwards towards the throat and head of the bird.

Mistle Thrush spots are much more rounded (see opposite). While you are taking in the detail of the spots, notice that on the breast they are set against a warm, sandy-brown background, whereas further down the background colour is a clean white.

If you see a Song Thrush in flight it will keep low, like a Blackbird, and it will hurry wherever it goes. If it must make a longer flight, the wing-beats will be fast and flickering, like those of a Blackbird. If you get a really good view of a flying Song Thrush you might be able to see that, under the wings – in the armpits, so to speak – the colour is yellowish-brown. This area is white in a Mistle Thrush.

Tip

Juvenile Song Thrushes, which appear from April to September, are readily distinguishable by their teardrop-shaped buff spots on the shoulders and down the back.

BELOW: *The Song Thrush is a retiring, cover-hug-ging species. Note its dark brown back and head, and its well-ordered breast spots against their sandy-brown background.*

BELOW: *The well-proportioned Song Thrush has a relatively larger head than the Mistle Thrush and just looks 'better designed'.*

Mistle Thrush

Distinguishing the Mistle Thrush from the Song Thrush is quite hard. Do not believe the books that say it's a cinch: it isn't. The problem is that the plumage differences are quite detailed and subtle, and the easiest way to tell these birds apart is by their shape, which takes confidence and experience.

However, unless you have a very large garden with a wide lawn, or live near fields, you probably won't see the Mistle Thrush very often. In contrast to the cover-hugging Song Thrush, which thrives in the suburban tapestry of small lawns and herbaceous borders, the Mistle Thrush prefers wide, open spaces. It will often feed in the middle of a playing field, allowing it to see danger coming. When frightened it does not make a dash for cover like the Song Thrush, but flies off to the nearest treetop, where it will wait until the disturbance clears. Its flight is very distinctive because, in contrast to both the Blackbird and Song Thrush, the bird follows a distinctly undulating course quite similar to that of a woodpecker.

Having said all that, if a Mistle Thrush unexpectedly turns up on a postage-stamp sized lawn, how can a good look clinch it?

Let's go for those important details first. First, look at the spots. In contrast to those of the Song Thrush, they are definitely not arranged in lines, but sprinkled about the breast. They are more

ABOVE RIGHT: *The Mistle Thrush stands tall and erect, often far from cover. The spots on its lower breast are rounder than those of the Song Thrush, clearly not arranged in lines – the bottom ones actually point downwards. Note how the 'ink has run' on either side of the breast.* BELOW: *Notice the Mistle Thrush's small head, long tail and pot belly.*

rounded than those of a Song Thrush, and, if anything, the ones on the lower breast 'point' down not up. All the spots are set against a white background (not a warm buff one), except a few that appear to coalesce into a cloudy spot on each side of the breast. No Song Thrush ever shows a dark patch here.

The next thing to consider is a potential minefield: colour. While Song Thrushes are dark brown on the wings and back, Mistle Thrushes are anaemically pale. At first sight this is not easy to judge, but if you can see that the rump of the bird is paler than the back, you have a good case for Mistle Thrush.

To more experienced birdwatchers, the Mistle Thrush's wing pattern is a giveaway. On the folded wing the flight feathers in the centre of the wing (the secondaries and tertials) have pale edges, together producing a clear pale patch of soft grey. When the bird takes flight, the underside of the wing is clearly white.

One further subtle but useful detail is that the Mistle Thrush has white sides to the tail, which swell into blobs at the tip. No other thrush displays this.

Tip

It's time to consider the Mistle Thrush's much-vaunted distinctive shape. The species is larger and heavier than the Song Thrush, and slightly larger than a Blackbird. In contrast to the neat, petite, evenly proportioned Song Thrush, the Mistle's tail is noticeably long, and its head small. The chest sticks out like a beer-gut, near the belly, giving the bird a proud, confident look, exaggerated by its habit of standing very upright and drooping its wings down a little.

Fieldfare

Having stated in my discussion of the Song Thrush that there are only two types of thrush in British gardens, I now need to qualify the statement by admitting that, in winter, a further two species are possible.

The thing is, they don't have 'thrush' in their name, and both are distinctive enough in colour and pattern to render confusion unlikely. However, strictly speaking, Fieldfare and Redwing (see opposite) are both members of the thrush family; so is the Blackbird.

The Fieldfare is the larger of the two so-called 'winter thrushes', lying midway between Blackbird and Mistle Thrush in size; it is larger than the former and smaller than the latter. It occurs in gardens during October–March, although it is usually much more regular in late winter, when the supply of berries out in the countryside begins to diminish. Fieldfares usually go around in flocks, often with Redwings.

Given a decent view, the Fieldfare is quite easy to identify. Its head is mostly smoky-grey, its mantle is a magical hue of velvet, and its lower back and rump are, once again, as grey as a thundercloud. The tail is all black, and, on the head, the Fieldfare has a white stripe over the

ABOVE: *This photograph shows off the ash-grey nape and rump of the Fieldfare very well.* **BELOW LEFT:** *Notice the fluffy white patch under this bird's wing, at the 'shoulder'. It's a distinctive feature, visible from a long way off.*

eye. In good light, it is a pretty appealing bird to look at.

The breast pattern is quite complicated – a bit like a hybrid between a Song Thrush and Mistle Thrush breast. The upper breast is streaked and soaked in warm ochre, rather like that of a Song Thrush. The lower breast is boldly patterned, not with spots but with chevrons. A very distinctive feature, shown by no other thrush and visible at great distance, is a nick of white feathering on the side of the breast next to the wing. This has the appearance of a tear in a smart piece of clothing.

When a Fieldfare flies, it shows white under the wing, like a Mistle Thrush. The flight is slightly undulating, but the wingbeats are oddly loose, giving the impression that the bird is not trying very hard to move forward. Bursts of flaps alternate with unsteady glides.

Tip

The male Fieldfare tends to show more extensive black peppering on its crown than the female.

Redwing

The smallest of the thrushes, the Redwing is about the size of a Starling. It visits gardens in the autumn and winter, any time from October to about March or April, and it usually does so in small groups.

The species' name is misleading because its wings are not red – at least, not on the side you see when they are folded. On their undersides, the wings have indeed been daubed with an attractive rusty-red, but you can only see this when the bird flies. Some colour, though, has 'leaked' onto the bird's flanks, and is readily seen as a large stain.

It is probably too much to ask that birds should always be named after their most prominent feature, but it is still frustrating to recount that, to identify the Redwing definitively, you need to look at the head, not the wing. Here, the Redwing exhibits a very strong pattern that almost suggests it has spent hours putting on make-up in the morning. It has a broad pale stripe over the eye and there is a slightly less obvious line going down the side of the face, bordering the throat. Even at great distance, the eyebrow is an instant recognition feature, which rules out the plain-faced Song Thrush.

It is also worth noting that the Redwing has neat black stripes going down its white breast – definitely not spots. Moreover, its bill is yellow with a black tip, unlike the less contrasting bill of the Song Thrush.

This is a small, compact thrush with a short tail. It flies in a different way to the other thrushes, with faster wingbeats, and looks extremely like a Starling in flight. It tends to fly above treetop height, something a Song Thrush rarely does (but Starlings habitually do).

Tip

By examining plumage details you can tell where your Redwing has come from. We receive plenty of Icelandic-breeding birds in Britain in the winter, and these have slightly darker upperparts than the more abundant Scandinavian birds; in addition, the streaks of the upper breast are more densely packed, almost coalescing. You can also easily pick out young (first-winter) birds from adults: these have pale edges to the secondary and tertial feathers and spots on the end of the latter.

ABOVE: *The Redwing's most distinctive feature is not the 'red wing' but its unmistakable pale eyebrow.* **LEFT:** *Redwings, in common with all thrushes, eat large numbers of berries in the autumn and winter.*

Blackcap

The Blackcap is a member of the warbler family, a group notorious for being difficult to identify. It's good to report, then, that this species is an exception to the rule, being very easy indeed. So long as you can see the smart skullcap, black in a male and toffee-coloured in a female, you should be fine. The species is about the size of a Great Tit.

Warblers as a rule are skulking birds that do not show themselves very often, and then usually only briefly. Apart from its frequent visits to bird tables in winter, the Blackcap behaves like this, too. It is also a fidgety bird, constantly moving from one branch to another within the foliage.

RIGHT: *Despite sharing the same name, the female Blackcap's skullcap is actually toffee-brown in colour.* **BELOW:** *It's hard to misidentify the male Blackcap: only the Marsh or Willow Tits (page 48) are remotely like it.*

The only likelihood of confusion is with one of the black-capped tits, particularly the Marsh Tit (see page 48). Note, though, that the Blackcap has a thinner bill, while the Marsh Tit shows a black bib and a contrasting white cheek, both lacking in the Blackcap.

Although in Britain as a whole the Blackcap is first and foremost a summer visitor to woods and forests, its visits to gardens are usually in wintertime, between November–March. Blackcaps that inhabit winter gardens are not our native breeding birds, which migrate south for the winter, but are, in actual fact, visitors from Germany.

Tip

One might be tempted to place the Blackcap within the pantheon of small brown birds, but a detailed look shows it to have a distinct grey cast, especially on the nape.

ABOVE: *Chiffchaff.* BELOW RIGHT: *Willow Warbler.*

Chiffchaff and Willow Warbler

These two Blue Tit-sized, olive-green warblers are so similar that we are treating them in the same section here. This should send the message that, if you don't want to, there is no need to try to tell them apart. At any rate, they are not very common in gardens except as migrants, appearing in small numbers almost anywhere between March–May and then again between August–October. Distinguishing them is a job for more experienced birdwatchers, but there is nothing to stop you trying.

There's no doubt, though, that the sight of one of these plain but likeable birds in your garden is pretty exciting. They are very much countryside birds, found in woodland or scrub, so their visit to a garden is always a bit special. In autumn, they often join flocks of tits moving through the neighbourhood. In spring, you have a good chance of seeing them in blossom trees and willows.

It only takes a half-decent view to confirm that these small birds are something other than Blue Tits. They are plainer, for a start, without the bold head markings of any tit. Their bills are thin and their bodies are slim, with moderately long tails that they flick and twitch. They move rapidly through the foliage – classic warbler behaviour – never staying still for long, as if they had itching powder on the tail. They do not show themselves easily – they don't visit bird tables, for example – so you'll have to follow the moving leaves carefully with your binoculars. Both species have weak, fluttery flight, very similar to that of a small tit.

Both the Chiffchaff and Willow Warbler are slightly paler below than above, and both have a pale eyebrow, or supercilium. This should distinguish them from other species of warbler, including the Blackcap.

A clue for telling this tricky pair apart with minimum effort is that, while feeding, the Chiffchaff wags its tail with great regularity. The Willow Warbler does it less often and less mechanically.

Tip

So, you want to tell these two warblers apart? Here are the best identification features, roughly in order of usefulness:
- Chiffchaff has dark or black legs; Willow Warbler has flesh-coloured legs
- Willow Warbler has an immaculate breast, which is either whitish or (in autumn) yellow; Chiffchaff has a slightly dusky breast that is more in keeping with, and provides less contrast to, the colour of its upperparts
- Willow Warbler has a flatter crown and a longer, more pronounced supercilium; Chiffchaff has a rounded crown and its supercilium is less obvious
- Willow Warbler has relatively clean cheeks; Chiffchaff's darker cheeks accentuate the lower part of its split eye-ring
- Willow Warbler is slightly longer-winged and longer-bodied than Chiffchaff

Goldcrest

If the question 'What is the smallest bird in Britain?' was asked on a quiz show, you can bet your bottom dollar that the contestant would most likely say 'Wren'. But he or she would be wrong. The Goldcrest is Britain's record-holder. For some reason, the public at large just don't seem to have heard of it.

This tiny bird is quite common in gardens, especially in winter. The sure-fire way to attract it is to have a coniferous tree in your garden – even a cypress will do. With its minute size and long, ultra-thin bill, the Goldcrest is adapted to hunt for food among needles. In winter, it often also forages in deciduous trees and herbaceous borders, so you can expect to receive a visit from time to time.

Identifying a Goldcrest is often easy because individuals are typically quite tame, going about their business just a few metres away from an entranced observer. Look for the small size, rotund shape, dark staring eye, short tail and pale double wing-bar. If you cannot make these features out, the behaviour often gives this bird away. It is nimble

and acrobatic and makes a habit of hovering briefly at the end of branches, like an impatient hummingbird – no other British garden bird does this, except for the occasional Coal Tit. The Goldcrest also flicks its wings constantly, and never stops moving. All in all, given a reasonable view, the Goldcrest is easy to identify and appreciate.

Tip

Both sexes of the Goldcrest have a yellow central crown stripe bordered by black on either side. In the male, the colour intensifies to orange on the nape, although this is often visible only when the bird raises its crown feathers in excitement.

Spotted Flycatcher

There is no problem with one part of this bird's name, but there's a very big problem with the other. It certainly catches flies, but it is not actually adorned with spots. Well, OK, the juveniles have a few spots on the back, but the adults – which have a right to a sensible name – do not.

To look at, this character should be just another small brown bird. Its plumage is hardly earth-shattering: it is plain brown above, paler below, and on the throat there are a few well-defined dark streaks. But the Spotted Flycatcher is exactly that – a character – a bird that is surprisingly easy to identify by behaviour alone.

For one thing, the Spotted Flycatcher takes up conspicuous perches; these may be on a post, the wires of a fence, the upper branches of a tree (especially if dead) or the top of a bush. Here, it will sit fairly motionless and then, very suddenly, it will dart into the air in pursuit of a flying insect, follow the latter's irregular path until captured, and then return, triumphant, to its original perch, or another nearby, and perhaps flick its wings once or twice as a mark of satisfaction. After another period of sitting motionless it will once again dash off in aerial pursuit, and continue like this until its hunger, or that of its chicks, subsides.

Other birds simply do not act like this. When chasing an insect, the Spotted Flycatcher is as agile as a Swallow: twisting, turning and hovering on its long, elegant wings. Yet it sits so still that it is easy to overlook.

These delightful birds are summer visitors to quite a number of gardens throughout the country. They arrive very late, in about the second or third week of May, and are usually on their way back to Africa when September arrives.

Tip

A close look allows you to appreciate the Spotted Flycatcher's distinctive shape: long, pointed wings; short black legs; a very large, rounded head; large eyes; an extremely broad and laterally flattened bill that gives the bird a wide gape; and small bristles (known as rictal bristles) on the side of the bill, which are probably touch-sensitive.

OPPOSITE TOP: *The tiny, round-bodied Goldcrest has an obvious dark, staring eye in a blank face.* **OPPOSITE BOTTOM:** *You don't often see Goldcrests on the ground, but this photograph does show off the black-edged yellow crown very clearly.* **LEFT:** *Spotted Flycatcher is hardly an appropriate name for this mousy-brown, streak-breasted bird. It often perches on wires like this, sometimes even low down on fences.*

Pied Flycatcher

A few gardens, mainly those to the west and north of Britain, are privileged to have Pied Flycatchers as summer residents. The sites most likely to be blessed are rural gardens adjoining deciduous woods, into which Pied Flycatchers can be attracted by putting up nest-boxes. These birds are inveterate users of artificial nesting sites.

Pied Flycatchers are small birds, not much larger than Blue Tits. The boldly marked males are easy to identify, with their stark black-and-white colouration. Females are more difficult and bear a passing resemblance to a female Chaffinch, but they are smaller, with shorter tails, cleaner white under-

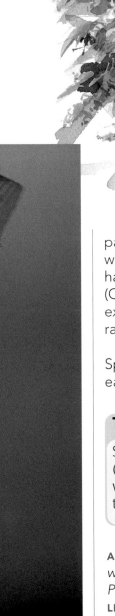

parts, a thin bill, and a much simpler, less messy wing pattern. They also have the flycatcher-like habit of making aerial forays to catch flying insects (Chaffinches do this as well, although not so expertly) and they habitually flick their wings and raise their tails.

Pied Flycatchers arrive in late April, earlier than Spotted Flycatchers, but they also depart very early. Most have gone by the end of August.

Tip

Sometimes Pied Flycatchers turn up in gardens on migration (as I know to my delight, writing this a few days after such a visit) so keep a look out for them. When fly-catching, they tend to change perches more frequently than Spotted Flycatchers.

ABOVE: *With its gleaming white breast and wing-patches, and jet black back, the male Pied Fly-catcher (lower bird) is easy to identify.*
LEFT: *The Pied Fly-catcher is recognisable by its white wing-patches.*

Blue Tit

One of the first birds people learn to recognize in the garden, the Blue Tit is dirt-common and often tame. It is a small, brightly coloured sprite with a yellow breast, a thin black stripe through the eye, and a bright cobalt-coloured crown. The crown has ultraviolet reflectance, and the 'sexiest' males have the brightest crowns, although only the birds can see this, not us.

Some Blue Tits, especially those that are worse for wear for any reason, may show the hint of a dark stripe running down the middle of the breast, but this is never as broad as the showy breast stripe of a Great Tit.

Tip

Juvenile Blue Tits may be seen between May–August. They have yellow, not white, cheeks, and this equally applies to Great and Coal Tits.

Long-tailed Tit

The shape of the Long-tailed Tit is alone enough to identify it. It is the only small bird with a long tail to be found in the garden, except for a wagtail, but a wagtail is a ground-living bird that walks on your lawn or drive or along your roof. Long-tailed Tits live in trees and bushes and move acrobatically through branches, never coming to the ground.

Typically, you will see Long-tailed Tits in small parties of 5–12 birds (sometimes more in late summer), often mixed in a flock with various other tits.

Tip

It is reasonably straightforward to separate adult Long-tailed Tits from juveniles. An adult has a whitish head with a dark stripe over the eye, and is washed pink on the back and underparts. A juvenile has a mainly sooty-brown side to the head, surrounding the eye completely; it lacks any pink colour in the plumage (see page 88). Juvenile Long-tailed Tits may be seen in the garden between late April and September.

ABOVE LEFT: *Adult Long-tailed Tit.* **BELOW:** *The yellow cheeks of this Blue Tit identify it as a juvenile.*

Great Tit

About the size of a Chaffinch, this is the largest tit that visits the garden and it should present few identification problems. It has a bold white cheek surrounded entirely by black and there is a broad black stripe down the centre of its breast, dividing the two sides. It also has a single white bar that runs across its wing.

This is the only species of tit in which males and females can be told apart with reasonable ease. The difference hangs on the black breast stripe and its definition. In a male, the stripe is broad and well-defined, continuing to be wide as it reaches down between the legs; in a female, the stripe is never so broad, and as it 'flows' down the breast it peters out like a dying river, leaving little trace between the legs.

Tip

Note that the Great Tit is the only tit that has obvious white sides to the tail. When it flies it has more powerful, less whirring wingbeats than other tits.

ABOVE: *On this female Great Tit the black breast-stripe peters out before it reaches the legs.* **LEFT:** *The black breast-stripe of the male Great Tit is broad and reaches down to the legs and beyond.*

Coal Tit

The Coal Tit is not sooty-black all over as its name might suggest, but it is not brightly coloured, either. Lacking any yellow or blue in its plumage, it looks like a black-and-white Great Tit or one which has been otherwise drained of colour.

This is the smallest of our tits, and it has several key features that make it easy to identify. For one, its black crown gives way to a finger of white on the nape, so that the back of its head has a pattern like the face of a Badger (well, something like that). Second, on its grey-brown wings there are two rows of neat white spots, which at a distance look like unbroken bars. Together with a brownish-yellow breast, this constitutes a unique package. This is the sort of bird that, once given a decent look, is easy to recognize.

RIGHT: *The highly agile Coal Tit is at home on hanging feeders.* BELOW: *You can just see the white nape that marks this Coal Tit out from other tits. Also note the large head and short tail, plus the two wing-bars (one quite hard to make out) made up from white spots.*

In most gardens Coal Tits are third in terms of abundance behind Blue and Great Tits. They are present all year in the countryside, but in gardens they often turn up only during the winter months, especially after Christmas.

Tip

Away from the bird table, it can be difficult to see a Coal Tit because this species often stays up in the treetops, especially among the branches of conifers. At a distance, it can be seen to be a dumpy, large-headed bird with a rather short tail. It is highly acrobatic, and, in contrast to the other tits, hovers fairly often (the Goldcrest does, too).

Marsh Tit and Willow Tit

There's something about the epithet 'Willow'. Two of the best-known tricky species pairs in Britain are the Willow Warbler and Chiffchaff, and the Willow Tit and Marsh Tit, the species in each couplet being famously hard to tell apart from one another. But the warblers are a piece of cake compared to the two tits!

Distinguishing Marsh and Willow Tits is so difficult that many birdwatchers, even highly experienced ones, just cannot and will not do it. So if you are in the habit of working through the Tip sections in this chapter, I suggest you tackle this one last.

Before saying anything more about the Marsh Tit, its idiosyncratic name must be considered. You see, against all logic, it simply does not occur in marshes: it is a woodland bird and quite a regular visitor to gardens. Don't worry about the origin of the name as the explanation is convoluted. Just ignore it.

Let's start by taking these two species together, and attempt to separate them from the other tits. This should be quite easy to do because although they are of similar shape and size to Blue Tits, they have quite different plumage. Many books draw a similarity to the Coal Tit due to their lack of bright colours, but this is not really a valid comparison: Marsh/Willow Tits lack the Coal Tit's two white wing-bars and its white nape, and both are more evenly proportioned in shape.

ABOVE: *Marsh Tit.* **BELOW LEFT:** *Willow Tit.*

One thing that often strikes you about Marsh and Willow Tits is how neat and tidy they always seem to look. The perfect black cap and trim bib are the equivalent of a top hat and bow tie. Apart from these two features and a whitish cheek, Marsh and Willow Tits are simply dark brown above and paler brown below. And that's all there is to it.

Both species are localized in distribution, and both are territorial. They simply do not occur in flocks like other tits, only as singles or pairs (except in late summer). Both are unadventurous in their travels, so if you don't already have one or both species in the garden, you should not expect ever to add them to your garden list.

Tip

Here are some important differences between these two tits:
- Willow Tit usually shows a pale panel in the middle of its wing, not shown by the plain-winged Marsh Tit
- Marsh Tit has a glossy cap (remember this as 'moist from the marsh'); Willow Tit has a matt black cap
- Willow Tit's black cap reaches further down onto the nape, and its bib is larger and more diffuse at the edges; Marsh Tit's cap is smaller and neater
- Willow Tit has slightly warmer brown colouration on the flanks, which may contrast with the colour of the belly, a feature not shown by the evenly-hued Marsh Tit
- Willow Tit has a larger head, with a slightly bull-necked appearance

Nuthatch

The Nuthatch has been imaginatively described as 'a Kingfisher that dived into detergent and washed off the iridescence of its plumage'. And you can see the point: it has the same large head, short tail, dagger-shaped bill, bluish upperparts and reddish underparts, but without the water bird's dazzling 'electric' sparkle. The Nuthatch is, moreover, a woodland species that lives in the trees.

As far as identifying the Nuthatch is concerned, that is just about all there is to it. Nothing else looks particularly like this bird. It regularly comes to bird tables and hanging feeders, and for the rest of the time hangs onto tree trunks, either upright or upside-down (see illustration). Nuthatches occur in gardens all year round, although they are often easiest to see in winter.

In flight, look for a dumpy bird with a large head and a short, blunt tail. The latter feature should eliminate the Lesser Spotted Woodpecker, which is of similar size but has a sharply pointed tail. When airborne, Nuthatches progress with strongly undulating flight, another characteristic that they share with woodpeckers.

Tip

It is possible to tell male and female Nuthatches apart. The male usually shows a deeper reddish-brown colour on the underparts than that shown by the female.

LEFT: *This is the typical head-down posture of the Nuthatch, which, combined with its shape, sets it apart from all other garden birds. Look at the large feet, too. On this bird there is little sign of a sharp contrast between the colour of the undertail and the buff colour of the breast and belly, suggesting that this bird is a female.*

Treecreeper

Many people's favourite, the Treecreeper is a small bird that is much easier to identify than to see. It is shy, well-camouflaged and quiet, and relies upon being overlooked for its safety and security. It knows only one way of living, and that is to climb up tree trunks vertically with a series of shuffling hops, like a mini-woodpecker. Its mouse-like progress, hugging close to the bark, makes it resemble a clockwork toy.

The Treecreeper's shape is unique. It has a fairly long and slightly down-curved bill and a stiff, straight tail that it uses as a prop in conjunction with clinging to the trunk with its feet. The Treecreeper does not always climb straight up, but follows the fissures in the bark. When it has reached a point of its choosing, it flies down in a tumbling flight and starts at the bottom of another tree, or even the same one again.

Not many gardens have Treecreepers, although a good number of these birds doubtless pass by households without being detected. If you have plenty of mature trees or even a wood adjoining your garden, keep a lookout for this little gem.

ABOVE: *The typical foraging style of the Treecreeper. Starting at the bottom of a tree, it works its way up the trunk, hugging it tightly, before flying down and starting at the base of the next tree.* **BELOW LEFT:** *The long, curved bill of the Treecreeper is ideal for probing into holes and fissures.*

Jay

The Jay is one of the garden's dandies. Daringly clad in pink, offset by sharp black and white and a sprinkling of kingfisher-blue on the wing, it cocks a snook at the crow family's reputation for producing birds with severe black plumage. As such, it is extremely easy to identify. Even if you do not see a visiting Jay well, the sight of its black tail and bright white rump – it is the largest woodland bird to have a white rump – will give it away as it flees.

Jays are present in gardens throughout the year. However, in summer they can be known to disappear into the canopy of large trees and be extremely secretive.

Tip

The Jay has a very distinctive flight, making it readily identifiable even at great distance. The rounded, fully extended wings are flapped to the full, then only half-flapped, and as a result the bird seems to make only faltering progress.

Magpie

With its bold black-and-white plumage and long tail, the Magpie is one garden bird that is instantly recognizable. It occurs in many gardens all year. It seems to be a poor flier, apparently needing to flap fast and frantically to keep itself airborne, giving the impression of flying into a headwind under perpetual threat of stalling.

Tip

An identification tip about a Magpie? Well, apparently, the longer the tail an individual Magpie has, the higher up the social scale it sits. Juveniles, with the shortest tails, are at the bottom of the heap.

ABOVE: *The four-colour Jay.* **OPPOSITE BOTTOM RIGHT:** *The two-colour Magpie – but note the iridescence on its wings and tail.*

Rook

Three members of the crow family that sometimes visit gardens are clad mainly in black: the Jackdaw, Carrion Crow and Rook. The Jackdaw is small and quite distinctive, but the Rook and Crow are very similar and cause birdwatchers a lot of problems. Beginners struggle with perched birds, and those with a great deal of expertise struggle with distant individuals in flight. So there's something for everyone here.

Much the easiest way to tell a Rook from a Crow is by the dirty white patch at the base of the former's bill, a soiled sheet of colour entirely lacking in the Crow's plumage or bare parts. A closer look will also reveal that, where it meets the bill, the Rook's forehead is very steep. The Crow shows a smooth incline from the peak of its crown down to the end of its bill, but the Rook appears to have received a bump on its head.

There are other differences, too. The Rook's plumage often shows a glossy, purplish sheen in good light, especially on the head and back, whereas the Crow's colouration is more solidly black. On the belly, the Rook's feathering becomes shaggy, hanging over the legs like an ill-fitting pair of shorts; the Crow is better turned

ABOVE: *A Rook flies to its nest with its throat bulging with food for its young.* **BELOW LEFT:** *With its baggy shorts, dirty-white bill and high crown, the Rook is easy to identify on the ground.*

out. Its belly feathers hug its thighs closely, like a pair of leggings.

The Rook is a less sinister-looking creature than the Crow. It has a more jaunty, waddling walk, rolling slightly from one side to the other. Now it sounds ridiculous, but someone once commented that the Carrion Crow moves around with a sinister air, whereas the Rook looks a bit more like your favourite auntie. For some reason, this works!

The majority of gardens don't receive visits from Rooks. These birds are colonial, and they only occur on or near to farmland with adjoining woods or lines of tall trees. They may commute some distance between one and the other and pass over gardens, but if your garden is deep in the suburbs or within a city, you probably won't see any Rooks.

Tip

In flight, the Rook progresses with slightly faster and fuller wingbeats than a Crow, giving a more supple action. But you'll need to see a good number of flying birds of both species before you can master the difference.

Carrion Crow

When people see Carrion Crows on their garden lawn, they often mistake them for Ravens, since they appear big and a bit frightening. But you are about as likely to find a Dodo on your lawn as a Raven. It's just a Crow in heightened perspective.

The Carrion Crow is the commonest member of its family in gardens. Its plumage is of unyielding black, and for good measure, its legs and bill are black, too. It carries a scowling, unfriendly, menacing expression. When walking, it sometimes skips forward, feet together resembling a vulture at a carcass. The bill is heavy and can be used as a blunt instrument. Its charms, then, tend to be well-hidden.

Carrion Crows are not, on the whole, sociable. Most are seen on their own or in pairs, but each neighbourhood is likely to support a non-breeding flock comprising mostly young birds, numbering a dozen or more individuals. Be careful not to assume that a gathering of large black birds is inevitably a flock of Rooks.

In parts of Scotland and in Ireland, the Carrion Crow is replaced by a very differently coloured variety of crow, the Hooded Crow. Far from being unrelentingly black, the Hooded Crow is pale grey on its nape, back and most of the underparts; the colour is like that of old, stale snow (see page 95).

Crows of both colour schemes have a powerful flight with deep, slow, deliberate wingbeats. They often fly high up and are capable of soaring if the fancy takes them, although they do this less often than either Rooks or Jackdaws.

Tip

On the theme of separating Rooks and Crows in flight, note that the Rook has a slightly longer, more wedge-shaped tail than the Crow, and very slightly narrower wing-tips. Where the wings join the body, they are slightly pinched in, but spotting this is a matter of fine judgment.

ABOVE : *The Carrion Crow (this individual is moulting) has a more square-ended tail than the Rook.*
BELOW: *The fearsome Crow is black all over and has a flat crown.*

Jackdaw

The Jackdaw is our smallest black crow, but that is not the easiest way to identify it. The real clincher is its small bill, which is much shorter than that of any other crow. In flight, when the size difference between black crows becomes a lot less apparent, the small bill remains as a beacon of reliable identification.

Jackdaws are distinctive when perched. Alone among black crows, they have a pale beady eye. They also have a grey nape, as if the back of their head has been sprinkled with ash, and this contrasts with the black forehead and crown. On the ground, they walk with a distinctly confident, jaunty step. A reasonable view will make all these features pretty obvious.

The flight is also distinctive because Jackdaws beat their wings much faster than the larger black crows – almost as quickly as a pigeon. When a Jackdaw soars it becomes apparent that its wings have less obvious 'fingers' on the end than the wings of a Carrion Crow or Rook.

Jackdaws are year-round residents in many gardens, but they always need access to nest-

holes nearby. These may be in mature trees, quarries or chimney pots, and ultimately this is what determines the status of Jackdaws in your area.

Tip

Juvenile Jackdaws, from July–September, lack the grey on the head found in adults, so they should be identified on the basis of shape and behaviour.

ABOVE: *A pair of Jackdaws, showing off their pale eyes and powdery grey 'shawls'.* **LEFT:** *Even when in flocks, Jackdaw pairs stay together.* **OPPOSITE TOP:** *The juvenile Starling is very different to the adult, lacking any iridescence or spots.* **OPPOSITE BOTTOM:** *The star-like pale spots that are sprinkled over the Starling's metallic plumage give the bird its name.*

Starling

The Starling has been in decline recently, but it is still an abundant bird in many gardens throughout the country. It's a great species on which to practise your observational skills as, although it sports a variety of different plumages, it never loses its distinctive character and identity.

At first sight, the Starling might be confused with the male Blackbird, since the plumage of the two birds is superficially similar and they both run about on lawns. But several things about the Starling stand out: it has a much shorter tail than the Blackbird; it has a sharp, spiky bill; it has pink legs; it has glossy, not coal-black, plumage, which is often adorned with spots; and, although boasting a yellow bill in summer like a male Blackbird, it lacks that bird's yellow eye-ring.

The behaviour of the two species is also quite different. Blackbirds move about lawns in stop-start fashion, pausing motionless in between little runs from point to point. Starlings, on the other hand, just keep wandering around in industrious fashion without stopping, and they have a high-stepping, jerky gait. When a Blackbird flies off, it goes straight to cover, low to the ground; when Starlings fly off, they lift into the air, often turning in an arc before returning again. Finally, Blackbirds are essentially loners, while Starlings are almost always seen in small parties commonly comprising 5–20 individuals.

Once you have worked all this out, your major pitfall will be juvenile Starlings. Although these have the same shape and habits as adult Starlings, they really do look completely different: when I saw my first one as a child, I was convinced I had discovered a new species. They are simply grey-brown all over, the colour of milky coffee that has been left to go cold, and there are no spots on them anywhere. Later in the season, from September onwards, they will begin to acquire a patchwork of spots to break the monotony of their tones, and in October they will resemble the adults. But juvenile Starlings are a pitfall for beginners.

Starlings have a very distinctive shape in flight: their wings are triangular. They fly on a level course, without the strong undulations shown by other birds of comparable size, such as the Great Spotted Woodpecker, yet they still alternate bursts of wingbeats with short glides.

Tip

In breeding plumage, male and female Starlings have similar plumage, but the male's yellow bill has a bluish-grey base, while the female's bill has light pink at the base, a delightful parallel to human etiquette.

Starlings in summer have glossy plumage with very few spots, but in winter chicken pox breaks out and the birds acquire pale spots all over their dark body. The white speckles on the black breast were thought to resemble the stars in the night sky, hence the species' common name.

House Sparrow

House Sparrows are still a dominant force in many British gardens, in spite of their well-publicized population declines in recent years. The fact is that if you have House Sparrows, your garden will probably be overrun with them; but if you don't, you don't, and you might never see them at all.

It can be hard to appreciate the humdrum things in life, and House Sparrows fall into this category. The male is actually quite a handsome bird, with a chestnut stripe that runs from behind the eye, widening at the nape, and a colourful and intricate wing pattern. The problem is that, just as some men simply don't wear suits well, the House Sparrow refuses to look neat and tidy. It often crouches with its belly feathers ruffled and as a result looks scruffy, as if its shirt was hanging out. The smoky grey on its crown, cheeks and under-parts, a colour that looks so perfect on a Dunnock, just makes it look grubby, and its potentially smartest feature, the black 'badge' on its throat and breast, is so diffuse at the edges that it has an untidy, unfinished look. The House Sparrow needs a makeover – where are Trinny and Susannah?

As for the female, she is the archetypal frump. She has the same problems in dress as the male, but lacks the compensation of any bold pattern-

ing. Look at a female House Sparrow and how do you start describing it? The only feature of note is a buff stripe running from behind the eye to the back of the head (it is narrower than the male's chestnut stripe). This, in fact, is very useful in identification.

The House Sparrow's flight style is unusual. Most small birds follow a smooth undulating path, flapping their wings a few times to go up, and closing them to go down. The House Sparrow follows a straight path, flapping all the time. It flaps so fast, in fact, that it looks rocket-powered – and is perhaps not in total control.

Tip

In winter, the male House Sparrow's black frontal badge disappears, leaving only a black bib. Most of its other bold features are also clouded by pale tips to new feathers grown in the moult.

ABOVE: *Boldly marked (in the male) but irredeemably scruffy – the House Sparrow personified.* **LEFT:** *The female House Sparrow is the ultimate small brown bird – but note the pale stripe behind the eye.*

Tree Sparrow

Similar plumage pattern, similar colours, and yet the Tree Sparrow is everything a House Sparrow is not: smart, petite, clean, and winsome. It is hard to explain why, although having a pale grey-brown breast with a few delicate darker streaks must help a bit. As mentioned above, some of us are made to be immaculate, and the Tree Sparrow is one of the birds in our gardens that is blessed in this way.

Nonetheless, it does require close scrutiny to pick the Tree Sparrow out from its downtown relative. Look especially at the head pattern of a brown cap, small black bib with clearly defined edges, white cheeks and neck collar, and a small black cheek spot. In addition, the Tree Sparrow is slightly smaller and more compact than the House Sparrow, and has a more rounded head.

Interestingly, once you have mastered this set of plumage features you have the Tree Sparrow in the bag. That's because the female looks identical to the male and the winter plumage is no different from summer plumage.

Tree Sparrows are very local birds and not many gardens have them. Those that do are mainly in rural areas of the Midlands and eastern England.

Tip

The Tree Sparrow is said to have even faster, more dashing flight than the House Sparrow. However, this is a fine judgment to make.

ABOVE: *The neat, well presented Tree Sparrow.* **LEFT:** *On Tree Sparrows look for the chestnut cap and black cheek-spot.*

Chaffinch

Most gardens play host to Chaffinches, especially in the winter. They are among the most common and widespread of all British birds. Only very urban areas are unattractive to them, and where they are present they often visit gardens in healthy numbers.

Superficially, a Chaffinch resembles a House Sparrow, or at least the female Chaffinch resembles the female House Sparrow. Both birds are roughly the same size, but the Chaffinch is the slimmer of the two, with a distinctly longer tail. It also shows a markedly peaked crown.

Furthermore, at all times and in all seasons, both sexes of the Chaffinch, whether perched or flying, always show a white patch on the shoulders, and House Sparrows don't. Say it aloud several times before you go to bed each night: 'Chaffinches have white shoulders'. It's good identification therapy.

In contrast to sparrows, Chaffinches also have a complicated wing pattern showing a lot of white and a touch of yellow; a pink or creamy-brown (not grey) breast; and white edges to the tail. The plain-faced female Chaffinch lacks the female House Sparrow's pale stripe behind the eye. The Chaffinch is longer-tailed than any other

finch, and tends to perch more horizontally and less vertically.

In truth, identifying a male Chaffinch in spring is a cinch, because it is decidedly handsome. In winter, the males are simply washed-out versions of their spring selves. At all times of the year they show a good deal of pink on the underparts, while the females are whitish-brown.

On the ground, where they habitually feed, Chaffinches usually hop, but they also have an odd shuffling walk accompanied by slight nods of the head, rather like a chicken.

Tip

Chaffinches fly with the usual undulating progress of all finches, but in the air the tail looks noticeably longer than that of the other species.

ABOVE: *Female Chaffinch.* **LEFT:** *A smart male Chaffinch in spring.* **OPPOSITE:** *The orangey wash to the Brambling's plumage fits in well with the colour of autumn leaves.*

Brambling

The Brambling is an uncommon winter visitor (October–March) to a few selected gardens. Do not try allowing your brambles to grow in an effort to encourage this bird, because its name is misleading and has nothing at all to do with the plant (it derives from 'branded' or 'brindled', meaning marked with spots or streaks). The Brambling is a seed-eater and will come to bird tables, almost always among flocks of Chaffinches.

Most people first spot the Brambling as a 'Chaffinch' that somehow looks different. And so it does, with an attractive orange wash to the shoulders and breast. When it flies, it shows a black tail and obvious white rump, in contrast to the Chaffinch's green rump. The bill is yellow with a black tip – quite different from the dull bill of the Chaffinch, while those aforementioned spots are found on the flanks, clustered as if in a rash. Male Bramblings have brighter orange on the breast than females, and more black on the head.

If your garden attracts a healthy flock of Chaffinches during the winter, make sure you search carefully for a Brambling amid the birds that have assembled.

Tip

A careful look will reveal that the Brambling has a shorter tail than the Chaffinch, with a more obvious fork.

Greenfinch

Greenfinches are extremely common and ought to be better known than they are. Most of us really only register the Greenfinch as a bullying visitor to garden feeding stations, but the habitat we provide near our houses, with its immense variety of different shrubs, trees and cultivated plants, is simply heaven for this broad-billed generalist. Even the much-hated Leylandii cypress is close to its heart.

The problem, of course, is that Greenfinches are the plain-looking ones among a family of sparkling beauties – think of Goldfinches, Chaffinches and Bullfinches, for example. They also look a bit like female House Sparrows, especially in their shape, and the comparison brings them down to the House Sparrow's perceived level of grubbiness. It's time that the Greenfinch was appreciated for what it actually is…

…And that is, a plump, short-tailed finch with a noticeably upright stance when perched on a branch or twig. It often adorns treetops, where it tends to look front-heavy. The male is a delightful apple-green, the sort of colour you associate with the leaves bursting out in spring, and the female is only moderately less pleasing. Both have a brilliant yellow wing-bar and sides to the tail, although these features are more extensive on the male. When a Greenfinch is perched, the bar goes along

the bottom edge of the wing and is very obvious; it looks a bit like a yellow line painted to stop people from parking. In flight, the Greenfinch's bulk and its short tail are both key features.

The other noticeable features of the Greenfinch are on its head and face. It has a large head and a thick, pale pink bill. Around the eye, especially on the male, there is a small black mask below a pale eyebrow, and this gives it a rather severe, frowning expression that is slightly menacing. One naturally looks for a tattoo somewhere, or at least a bit of body piercing...

Streaks are a hot topic in finch identification. The male Greenfinch stands out by having none at all. The female, however, is subtly streaked both on the back, and, even more faintly, on the underparts (see Siskin).

Tip

Beware of the juvenile Greenfinch: a pitfall for the unwary. That's because it is heavily streaked with neat 'pencil' marks on the breast and back, and it hardly shows any yellow on the wings and tail. Look for the pale bill, and tread carefully.

ABOVE LEFT: *The aggressive look of this Greenfinch, with its thick bill and 'frowning' expression, is fairly typical.* **BELOW:** *The female Greenfinch is duller in colour than the male, and has less yellow on its wing-bars and tail.*

Goldfinch

This is not a bird that is likely to cause any identification problems, since it has a unique plumage. Happily, it is a regular visitor to many gardens, especially in spring and summer.

The only possible difficulty is provided by the young Goldfinch, which lacks the adult's distinctive head markings. The fact is, though, that youngsters are almost always closely accompanied by adults when they appear in July, August and September, so they can be identified, if you like, by proxy. However, if you do see a juvenile on its own, look for the brilliant yellow and black wing pattern, and notice that the head is of similar colour to that of thistledown, the Goldfinch's favourite food-plant.

Tip

In summer, the Goldfinch's wings and tail look almost black, but from late autumn onwards a line of white spots appears on the tips of the primary flight feathers, and the tail acquires white dots, too.

ABOVE: *The sight of Goldfinches coming to garden feeders is becoming more frequent.* **BELOW:** *Adult Goldfinch.* **BELOW RIGHT:** *The juvenile Goldfinch lacks the distinctive head markings.*

Siskin

A Siskin in the garden is a bit of a rite of passage for the home birdwatcher. These Blue Tit-sized finches are now a regular sight on hanging bird feeders almost throughout Britain, usually turning up in late winter. If you watch your feeding stations carefully enough, you will probably see one in the end.

Although perhaps closest in plumage to the Greenfinch, they are dwarfed by them. They also have a habit of feeding upside-down – something that Greenfinches do much more reluctantly. The Greenfinch's bill is broad and heavy, while the Siskin's is thin and sharp.

Male Siskins are handsome and distinctive creatures; females, are less obvious than their male counterparts. Look carefully at the wings and note that, in complete contrast to the Greenfinch, the yellow bar of the Siskin goes across the wing, not along its edge. There is the hint of a second yellow bar near the shoulders, too. This wing pattern is much more complicated than that of the Greenfinch.

ABOVE RIGHT: *The female Siskin lacks the head marking of the male, but note the yellow wing bar across the wing and the heavy streaking on the flanks.* **BELOW:** *The male Siskin is very smart, especially in spring.*

The other easy distinction from the Greenfinch is the presence in adults of heavy streaking, especially on the flanks. There are some streaks on the Siskin's grass-green back, too, and these are much more sharply defined than those on the female Greenfinch.

Tip

You probably won't receive a visit from juvenile Siskins, which are present from July to September, unless Siskins are breeding nearby, in which case you probably live in Scotland. They are strongly streaked on the back and underparts, and show a stronger wing pattern than a juvenile Greenfinch.

Linnet

It is debatable whether the Linnet deserves a place in a book like this, since it is a bird of weedy fields, farmland and commons, and only occasionally pops in to rural gardens. It is, however, often confused with the Redpoll (see below), which is a more regular garden visitor.

Bird artists enjoy painting Linnets because they can splash brilliant crimson liberally onto the page, something they don't often have a chance to do with British birds. The problem is that only males in breeding plumage sport the bright colours, and the amount of red varies between individuals. Females and non-breeding males are not colourful at all.

Look, then, for the white bar down the edge of the wing; the very small, grey bill; the greyish head; and, more useful than you might expect, the pale patches around the eye and on the cheek. Linnets are quite long, slim birds, and their narrow tail has white sides to it.

Tip

Linnets will probably not use your feeders or bird table, and they won't feed in the trees; Redpolls do both these things. They do perch on bush-tops, usually in small flocks, and take flight at the slightest provocation.

ABOVE RIGHT: *The raspberry coloured forehead of the Redpoll is its best-known feature, but the buff-coloured wing bar is just as important.*
LEFT: *A pair of Linnets in spring: male (bottom), female (top).*

Redpoll

The Redpoll is not very common, but it wanders widely and is worth looking out for in any garden, especially if there are birch trees around. It is an irregular user of hanging feeders or other feeding stations.

This is a small, streaky finch, about the size of a Blue Tit, and it would be readily written off as another little brown job, except for two distinctive features: first, all birds of any age or sex have a little black bib surrounding their absurdly small yellow bill; and second, every individual has a raspberry-red patch on its forehead. In spring, the male sports a substantial splodge of the same colour on its breast, and it makes a fine sight indeed.

Redpolls often join forces with Siskins and move around in mixed flocks. These two kindred spirits can look surprisingly similar, especially since the Redpoll and the male Siskin both have a black bib. However, the Redpoll has a single buff-coloured wing-bar, instead of yellow wing-bars like a Siskin. This is an unexpectedly useful distinction.

Tip

Redpolls are variable in size and colour. If you are lucky, you might receive a visit from a continental Redpoll, larger than our breeding one and with pale, powdery plumage.

likely to be visited occasionally. They feed on buds and blossom in early spring, and also increasingly visit hanging feeders.

When distinguishing the sexes, think about fruit. The male's breast is brilliant cherry-red, and the female's is a sort of pinkish-brown, like a plum. Both sexes have black wings with a single white bar, a black tail, a grey back and a jet-black cap that covers the eye and meets the black bill. The thick bill and rounded crown create an even curve over the forehead.

Bullfinches are easy to identify when flying away because of their black tail and prominent white rump. Since they are painfully shy, this is the view you are likely to get.

Yellowhammer

The Yellowhammer is one of those borderline species that often occurs in gardens but is not a garden bird. For example, you are most likely to receive Yellowhammers if you live near a farm or hedgerow, and you definitely won't find them if you are in a suburb or a city. This could change. One day, perhaps, Yellowhammers will follow other seed-eating birds from farmland into the garden on a regular basis, and delight us all. But for now they are peripheral characters in gardens.

Pretty ones, though. Yellowhammers are, at their best, stunning birds. Males have a brilliant buttery-yellow head and breast, which are almost canary-like, and both sexes have a rump of the richest chestnut. They are about the size of a Chaffinch, with a comparably long tail.

Male Yellowhammers are highly unlikely to cause identification problems, but females are

Bullfinch

People starting birdwatching quite often mistake a brightly coloured male Chaffinch for a Bullfinch, especially when the sun shines on a Chaffinch's pink breast and makes it look crimson. But once you see a real Bullfinch, you'll know it's the real thing. It just looks different – much plumper and with a fatter chest – and it is somehow silky and smart. In other words, you could say that the Bullfinch belongs in places where you cannot get in without a tie.

Bullfinches are widespread in Britain and wander widely: most gardens with a fruit tree or bushes are

ABOVE: *Content among the blossom, a male (top) and female (bottom) Bullfinch.* RIGHT: *The unmissable white rump of the Bullfinch is a good field mark.*

a bit sparrow-like. They do, however, have an unmistakable yellow wash to their plumage, and in contrast to House Sparrows, they are heavily streaked on the breast.

ABOVE: *No other garden bird has the bright yellow face of the male Yellowhammer (above, with female below) – but beware an escaped canary!*
RIGHT: *Superficially sparrow-like, the Reed Bunting has a longer tail with obvious white outer feathers. It's forever twitching its tail, too.*

Reed Bunting

Gardens are not good places for buntings because they subsist mainly on grass seeds, and most grasses in gardens are cut short. Nevertheless, the Reed Bunting is an uncommon but increasing winter visitor to places where food is put out regularly. You are likely to see one if your garden is close to a pond or other marshy area, or even heathland.

The Reed Bunting is about the same size as a sparrow, and it has a similar streakiness to its plumage, but there are several important differences. Reed Buntings have much longer tails than sparrows, and these have obvious white sides.

When you watch a Reed Bunting, it actually reminds you of this difference due to its habit of continuously twitching its tail.

A male Reed Bunting is quite easy to identify in the breeding season, with its smart black head and white collar. In the winter, though, it becomes more similar to the female. At this time, look for the distinctive pale 'moustache' that runs down the side of the cheek, beginning at the base of the bill. Bordered by black on either side, this is the Reed Bunting's second most important field mark.

Tip

In autumn, the smart black head and throat of the male Reed Bunting is lost under duller feathering. The relevant feathers are pale at the tip, but black just inside the tip. As the feathers begin to wear, the tips are rubbed off and the black is exposed once again, just in time for the breeding season. Since the abrasion of feathers happens at a slightly different rate for each bird, male Reed Buntings in early spring show everything from a brown to a black head.

Chapter 2

Watching Birds

Our everyday birds provide us with a great deal to watch and see, and even discover. We do not need to go to Borneo to see something interesting happening, or even something new. Much new information has been uncovered about even our most familiar birds in the last 30 years, and not all of it by scientists. For example, only recently Long-tailed Tits have been seen coming to hanging feeders for the first time and consuming fragments of nut. We used to think that these tiny birds were entirely insectivorous in winter, but now we know better. Or perhaps the birds have recently acquired a taste for nuts? Whatever the reason, this discovery was made in a garden, not in a laboratory, and by someone who just loved watching birds, not a specialist.

ABOVE : *A Kestrel hovering.*
OPPOSITE: *Bullfinch.*

The moment you sit by a window and watch the comings and goings of the birds, you are entering into another world – one ripe for enquiry. I am not suggesting that you get out pen and pencil and start writing down all the details of what you see, but I do recommend that you really watch. Keep your gaze fixed on one bird – each of the small, apparently incidental movements it makes could have great significance. Who knows, perhaps you will see something special or unusual? And even if you don't, you will soon get a feel for how the bird acts and what makes it tick. This chapter describes and illustrates many of the key behaviours and characteristics of a selected range of garden birds. You will not see them all, and you will observe some things that are not included here, but hopefully it will encourage you to take a closer look at what your birds are doing.

A Note about Disturbance

It is all very well watching the birds in your garden, but please remember that they are wild and should not be disturbed if at all possible. In particular, be sparing about your visits to nests and nest-boxes.

Grey Heron

Grey Herons are among those birds the lifestyle of which can be summed up in a moment of observation. You see them standing by your pond, peering down, waiting for the appearance of a fish to stir them into action, and that's essentially what they do all day. The harpoon-like strike is fast and easy to miss. It is like a goal in a football match: a moment that defines the whole point of the exercise, but blink and it's over.

The scientists who worry about these things have given names to the slight refinements of a heron's technique. Sometimes herons just wait motionless in the water, and the powers that be have called this 'Standing'; sometimes herons wander around the water's edge, and this has been assigned the term 'Walking Slowly'. At times, scientists can be an imaginative lot!

Despite appearances and expectations, herons do not actually impale fish in their bill – they only grab. However, should the fish be so impertinent as to wriggle, they will despatch it with a few well-aimed blows. It is raw and violent, a grubby garden drama by the pond-side.

Sunning

On warm days you might catch a particularly interesting behaviour in the garden: a heron sunbathing. This is not the usual Blackbird-on-the-lawn fare, but a very unusual posture in which the bird stands tall, spreads out its wings and directs them downwards, rather as though the bird was readying itself to catch a beach ball. Sunning is extremely good for the flight feathers, helping to keep them in shape.

BELOW: *A Grey Heron sunning.* **OPPOSITE:** *Sparrowhawks often pluck their prey on the ground, especially if it is heavy and cannot be carried off easily.*

Sparrowhawk

However well we may know the Sparrowhawk as a predator of birds in the garden, it can still give us a start to see one in action; it can even be upsetting. For some reason we garden bird enthusiasts tend to side with the smaller, weaker customers at our bird feeders, and seeing them being picked off by what is clearly an efficient predator can be an insult to our sensibilities.

Nonetheless, if you do see a Sparrowhawk strike, it is hard not to be impressed. If you consider what mobile prey it is compelled to catch – flighty creatures that are used to danger and are always on the alert – then at least you can admire its persistence and skill. Every Sparrowhawk attack is premeditated: the birds watch their quarry carefully before setting off on an ambush, and they usually make a concealed approach, using one of your hedges or part of your house as cover until the last moment. Only a small proportion of attempts succeed, perhaps one in seven. So a predatory life may seem easy, but in reality it is far from a breeze.

It is actually much easier to observe a Sparrowhawk in flight than when it is paying a visit to your 'fast-food restaurant'. It will frequently soar over rooftops in a wide circle, searching the ground below it. The trick is how to recognize it as a Sparrowhawk. Watch or listen to the reaction of birds around you: some will dive for cover, others will give high-pitched, drawn-out warning calls, and still others will fly in circles around the hawk. This is a typical response to this dangerous bird's presence; there will be no such rumpus with a Kestrel.

More intimate encounters with a Sparrowhawk are rare, but they do occur from time to time. You might, for example, see one of them using your garden fence as a plucking post: holding a lifeless body down with its talons and causing a shower of feathers as it plucks away methodically. Or you might even see the predator 'mantling' over recently caught prey, spreading its wings gargoyle-like and ruffling its feathers: this is a threat display to claim ownership of the corpse. If you see this, you should count yourself lucky.

Kestrel

This bird of prey was once commoner than the Sparrowhawk in gardens, but things have changed dramatically in recent years. Despite this state of affairs, the Kestrel still patrols gardens and if your bird feeders are attacked by a predatory bird, you cannot discount it. Some Kestrels use the same hunting tactics as Sparrowhawks – an ambush and strike – to procure their prey, although their preferred technique is hovering.

BELOW: *Flying on-the-spot above ground, the Kestrel keeps it head absolutely still so that it can spot small mammals below. Only Kestrels do this; Sparrowhawks never hover.*

Hovering

Kestrels are famed, and rightly so, for holding their position above the ground by flying into the wind – that is, hovering. With head down, wings flapping, tail fine-tuning, and body kept perfectly still, a Kestrel watches the ground below, mainly for small mammals and worms. Recently, it has been shown that Kestrels can see trails of urine made by voles and mice, detecting them in the ultraviolet spectrum. That is quite a thought – to have your urine give you fatally away!

Black-headed Gull

The Black-headed Gull tends to be an aerial bird in the context of the garden, always flying over. As such you will not see much exotic behaviour, but there are a few telling things to watch out for.

If you live inland you might notice that the gulls are present for most of the year, but not in spring between April–July. That is, of course, because they spend that time at their colonies on the coast or at freshwater marshes, and they should really be there until at least August. If you see a returning gull in July, it will probably be an individual that failed to breed, or one that is still too young to pair up.

Catching Insects

In August, you may witness the Black-headed Gull's adaptability. Every year on a hot day a big event occurs in gardens – ant-swarming day. This is the day that winged ants emerge in enormous numbers and fly around in an attempt to find a mate – a sort of insects' Mile High Club. The air becomes thick with emerging and flying ants, and many dexterous garden birds such as House Martins, Swifts, Spotted Flycatchers, Starlings and even House Sparrows make aerial sallies to nab them. High above the rooftops, Black-headed Gulls join in. They swoop and soar in excited groups, snapping up what they can like shoppers on the first day of a sale. Sadly for them, this particular event really is for one day only, and the ants return to their terrestrial lifestyle.

Commuting

In the last 50 years, the number of reservoirs and inland waters has vastly increased in Britain, and at the same time gulls of various kinds have become more and more accustomed to living hand in hand with people. Over the years, the gulls have settled upon an agreeable daily rhythm, spending the day feeding on playing fields, rivers or rubbish tips, and the night settled on large bodies of water, safe from land predators.

This is such a perfect lifestyle that it has become as much a part of gulls' lives as the plod to and from work of the hard-pressed human commuter, and it has become commonplace for the garden birdwatcher to witness streams of gulls flying between their places of work and rest as the light fades. They often fly in V-formation, in preoccupied silence, and they can make a spectacular sight as wave after wave passes over, especially against the setting sun. If gulls are ever beautiful, it is now.

Formation Flying

You might, incidentally, ask why birds assume these eye-catching formations. Canada Geese do the same thing, although much more noisily, and migrating birds fly in Vs as well. The physicists tell us that flying immediately behind the wing-tip of another bird enables an individual to take advantage of vortices of rising air, giving it lift and saving energy. It thus makes flying more efficient. That's great, you might think, unless you are leading the group, in which case you gain no advantage at all. But bird flocks do not have 'leaders' as such, and all the individuals in a flock change places at regular intervals.

ABOVE: *Gulls often adopt V-formation on their commuting flights.* **BELOW LEFT:** *The intelligent Herring Gull has learned that, if you drop shells on to a hard surface, they break open.*

Herring Gull

Gulls are intelligent creatures and can adapt their feeding behaviour to cope with a wide variety of situations. This is perfectly demonstrated when a bird flies up high with an implacable shellfish in its bill, only to drop it onto a hard surface to break it open. You might have seen gulls do this on beaches.

This is intentional behaviour but it might have unintentional consequences. There are many instances in which broken windows and other damage, initially put down to human vandals, have actually turned out to be caused by Herring Gulls dropping hard objects on to what must have resembled a suitable surface. One day – wait for it – a gull will drop a shellfish on a human head, and litigation will follow...

Collared Dove

Before delving into the private life of the Collared Dove, a few words about its recent history are appropriate. Its coos may seem to be a permanent fixture in the suburban landscape, but this was not always so. Before the mid-fifties, not a single Collared Dove had ever been recorded in Britain. But, at the end of a population surge through continental Europe that radiated out from the Balkans – and, before that, the Near East – the empire-expanding Collared Dove finally crossed the English Channel in about 1952 and fell in love with burgeoning suburbia. Now, 50 years later, having found an unoccupied niche, the Collared Dove is here to stay, with a countrywide population of about 300,000 pairs. By any standards, that is an impressive rate of colonization.

Not everyone has quite caught on. A very English furore was stirred up a few years ago when BBC Radio dramatized extracts from Gilbert White's celebrated book The Natural History and Antiquities of Selborne, published in 1789. The broadcast was up to the BBC's usual high standards, but somebody had the bright idea of replacing the usual theme tune with a wild track recorded in Selborne, Hampshire. There, among the Robins and Blackbirds, the mischievous coo of a Collared Dove could be heard. And in the context of the broadcast, of course, it was in the village about 200 years too early! Correspondence flew back and forth.

where it started, or another perch nearby. It rides an invisible helter-skelter, climbing up the 'inside' and sliding down the 'outside'. Having performed this simple up-and-down display, the Collared Dove will give a few bursts of its party-trumpet call, to add a bit of extra effect, and then resume a bout of perch-bound cooing.

In common with all pigeons and doves, Collared Doves pair for life and are more faithful to their mates than many other garden birds – good reason to appreciate them, if you can. Doves practise a variety of mutual displays to demonstrate togetherness, but often they simply sit side by side, huddled close together as if they were sitting on a sofa. At times they will indulge in preening, each bird nibbling the feathers of the other in a ceremony analogous to chimpanzees de-lousing their nearest and dearest. Tending to the feathers of another bird is called allopreening. The term may derive from the Latin allo for 'the other', but one cannot easily resist the thought that the doves must be saying soothing 'allo's' to one another.

Do not be surprised if you find a Collared Dove sitting on a nest at a strange time of year, such as January. So long as there is plenty of food around, seasons to these birds seem to be immaterial. They may raise five broods, or even more, in a single calendar year.

Spirals in the Air

The most eye-catching form of behaviour you will see from a Collared Dove is its territorial flight display. Starting from an elevated perch, such as a roof or aerial, the dove will flap its wings fast to gain height, rise at a steep angle and then, when it has deemed that the height is right, spread its wings out and glide down in a long spiral back to

RIGHT: *The showy, spiralling display-flight of the Collared Dove.*

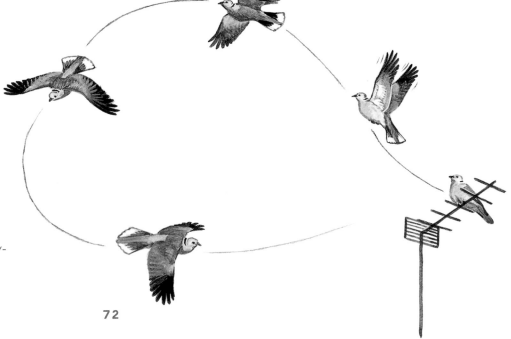

Woodpigeon

Woodpigeons are theatrical creatures and carry out all sorts of interesting behaviour that is easy to see. They even know how to make an entrance. They come in to the garden, land on a perch and lift their tail up towards their back in an exaggerated wag. At first it looks as though the tail has retained its forward momentum and the bird is lifting it so as not to overbalance. But it's more of a wave than a wag. It tells the other pigeons nearby that the bird is back where it belongs, and is therefore a deliberate message.

Territorial Woodpigeons have a display flight equivalent to the spiralling of a Collared Dove. It is a very common sight in gardens everywhere, and you are bound to have seen it before. The bird takes off from a perch, gains altitude with a few strong flaps, claps its wings sharply together, and then stalls in mid-air. Its momentum takes it forward and then gravity tugs it down until it regains control by resuming flapping, all the while flying in the same direction. The big difference between a Collared Dove display and a Woodpigeon display is that the Collared Dove performs over a small area and usually lands near the point at which it took off. The Woodpigeon, on the other hand, takes off from one place and heads for another, performing its routine en route. It is almost like an athlete running towards a vaulting horse, performing acrobatics over it and landing on the mat.

Water Features

If you have a pond in your garden, or provide a bird bath, you will probably have seen pigeons coming to drink. Whether or not you realized it, pigeons can drink like no other birds, for alone among our garden residents they are able to suck. Other birds practise the 'scoop and tilt' method of drinking, scooping up water in their bill and letting it drain down the throat: they are not able to suck.

Although one might guess that sucking helps pigeons to take in a lot of water in one go, it apparently is no more efficient for drinking than any other method. It is thought, however, that sucking enables pigeons to drink from very small sources of water, such as the little basins made by leaves, which would spill more easily if a bird tried to scoop water from them.

If the warmth of the summer in your garden is disturbed by a shower of rain (and let's face it, this does happen), take a glance towards your rooftop and you might catch sight of a Woodpigeon 'rain-bathing' – a real treat. The bird wallows in the downpour, holding on tight with its feet as it lifts one wing up and over the body, as if it was receiving an anti-perspirant spray. Once the rain has trickled down one 'underarm', the bird lifts the other wing and exposes the other side. Evidently, for a Woodpigeon, this is heaven.

BELOW: *A Woodpigeon drinking. It is among just a handful of birds that can suck up water.*

Pigeon Milk

Not all of the Woodpigeon's most interesting behaviour is so readily seen. You might know that pigeons are also unique among birds in the way that they feed their young. We are all familiar with the image of the hard-pressed Blue Tit making hundreds of trips a day to bring caterpillars to its young, or of a Blackbird with its bill full of wriggling worms. Woodpigeons circumvent the hard work involved by feeding their young on milk.

The manufacture of the milk takes place internally, within the pigeon's crop. The nutrients from the adults' meals are passed into cells in the lining of the crop, and these break off to make a sort of curd that is then regurgitated straight into the youngsters' throats. This acts rather like spinach on Popeye – the young pigeons grow very quickly into vigorous squabs, and, almost in the blink of an eye, into fecund factory-breeders.

ABOVE: *A Woodpigeon revels in a shower of rain.*
BELOW: *The wing-clapping display-flight of the Woodpigeon.*

Feral Pigeon

Do not ever underestimate the Feral Pigeon. It might be too common for your liking, or too lazy, or it might take too much of the food you have reserved for more attractive and 'worthy' species. But this bird is a jewel, a real marvel of the garden. Remember that Superman spent most of his time in the guise of Clark Kent; the Feral Pigeon, grubby in outlook but wondrously gifted, is much the same.

When you look at the Feral Pigeons in your garden, with their potpourri of colours and patterns and universally clueless demeanour, you must roll back the veil of your prejudice. Pigeons, you should realize, can do a great number of things you cannot do. For a start, they have the ability to predict the weather; scientists have discovered that they have the capacity to detect minute changes in atmospheric pressure, certainly enough to tell when a cold front is approaching, for example. So they do not need weather charts or the Met Office; they have it all in their heads.

Pigeons can also hear things we cannot, and to that extent there is a real analogy to Superman with his superhuman senses. The human ear is quite good at hearing high frequencies, but not low ones; we can pick up frequencies down to about 20Hz and no further. But a pigeon can hear down to 1Hz, which means that it can enter a whole realm of hearing that is simply not detectable to us: it will be aware of things like distant winds, storms at sea, the jet stream, and so on. While stuffing themselves on your bird table, a couple of pigeons could, for example, quite possibly be listening to a thunderstorm in Germany.

That's to say nothing of a pigeon's fabled powers of navigation. Feral Pigeons are simply gone-wild versions of carrier pigeons and racing pigeons, so they can navigate equally as well as birds that live in lofts. A racing pigeon once flew from the Channel Islands to Brazil unaided, a distance of 7,588 kilometres (4,743 miles), and there are countless other recorded instances of similar, if less spectacular, feats. On your roof or in your local park are birds with the same capacity for pinpoint travel as these – they are nothing less than navigational computers.

Pigeons can orientate themselves using the Sun, and can also reference their position using the Earth's magnetic field (another thing humans cannot do). They can remember landmarks, and probably even smells. And to motor them along, they have powerful flight muscles, which take them well above 70 kilometres per hour (44 miles per hour). Let's face it: compared to pigeons we are really quite inadequate.

BELOW: *The sight of pigeons flying in tight circles is often a sign that there is a predator about – like this Sparrowhawk.*

Racing Circuits

Hopefully, by now, you are humbled enough to watch your Feral Pigeons' behaviour. If you live in a built-up area you are quite likely to see a flock of pigeons flying around in a wide circle or arc. Such birds are probably on exercise, having been released from their loft for a bit of training. By going round in circles they can learn the landmarks around their 'home', and also fix their various co-ordinates prior to their next homing attempt. As you watch them, be amazed at all the information they must be processing; it is enough to make your own head spin.

Feral Pigeons also fly around in circles for another reason, and that is when there is danger in the skies. When a soaring Sparrowhawk or Kestrel is sighted by a member of the avian community, most garden birds dive for cover. But not Feral Pigeons: they take off and fly as a flock towards the predator, keeping in tight formation. By circling around the danger, keeping just out of reach, they might be attempting to confuse or irritate it. Or perhaps they are simply showing that they are too fit and healthy, and too street-wise, to make chasing them worthwhile.

The flight display of a Feral Pigeon is disappointing in comparison to the artistic efforts of its near-relatives. It flies in a circle and makes the odd wing-flap, gliding *en route* with its wings held up in a V. And that's about it.

BELOW: *A Woodpigeon in action.* **OPPOSITE:** *The Tawny Owl may act like a giant Blackbird at night, hunting worms on your lawn, especially in wet weather.*

Give your Pigeons a Score

This may seem like a totally daft project, but I'll try anything to help you appreciate your pigeons, since I believe that they are fantastic, underrated members of the garden bird community.

The display flights of the Collared Dove and Woodpigeon are easy to see and involve quite simple manoeuvres that can be easily recognized. The Collared Dove, for example, performs a lift, a stall and a spiral, while the Woodpigeon includes a lift, a clap and a forward roll. You can be sure that, within this framework, there is room for individual variation, for an extra flourish on a good day, and for a short-cut on a bad day.

The object of this exercise is to watch your performers and grade them. You could, for example, score the Collared Dove according to the following:

• Two points each for including a lift, stall and then spiral (to a maximum of six points)

• In the lift, a series of bonus points according to how high the bird goes

• In the spiral, extra bonus points for how perfect the circuits are and whether the wings move at the tip

• Further points for the landing, according to how clean it is or whether the bird has to adjust its position

• Finally, another bonus point if the bird goes on to perform another display straight away, before it lands

You have got the idea now, so do the same for the Woodpigeon. It's silly but fun, and will make you watch pigeons.

Tawny Owl

To see a Tawny Owl at all is difficult enough, so observing one indulging in interesting behaviour may seem a step too far for the household bird-watcher. But, if you have owls nearby and you can watch an area illuminated by street lamps or by garden floodlights, you might be lucky and see a hunting bird in action.

Owls obtain their food by a variety of methods, but the most frequent goes by the name of 'perch and pounce'. It is an apt description, since the owl just sits on an elevated perch and watches or listens for movement below. If something stirs, the hunter drops down and grabs it with its talons, and, if necessary, administers a fatal bite. It sounds easy and it probably is. Over the years an owl gets to know its territory well, and susses out the best perches for different meteorological conditions.

Tawny Owls don't always catch food by this method. They often fly low over the ground in hunting flight, for example, simply flopping straight down on to prey. On other occasions an owl will wander over your lawn in search of earthworms, and it might even raid your pond for tadpoles or fish – all under cover of darkness, of course. You probably blamed the heron.

Apparently, Tawny Owls show peaks of activity in their hunting throughout the night. They hunt a lot around dusk and again at dawn, and then even more so in the two hours either side of midnight. This is their favourite time. When it is damp and drizzly they may have to hunt all night because the sound of rain affects hunting by ear and the moon is obscured by cloud.

Owls are famous for their ability to see in the dark, but, remarkably, it has been shown that their vision is actually no better than ours. So, if you tip-toe out into the garden at night and let your eyes become accustomed to the unfamiliar shadows, you can imagine you are an owl with unusual confidence and wonder at these birds' sheer expertise. They have other attributes to help them, of course. Their hearing is much better than ours, and it is tuned to be most sensitive at a frequency similar to the squeaks and rustles made by small rodents.

Swift

The aerial Swift is an easy bird to watch and is one of the dominant characters of the skies. Since it lives aloft in full view of the ground, you can see plenty of interesting behaviour while you are sitting comfortably in a deckchair on your lawn. And because the Swift is a fair-weather bird, you'll have to conduct your observations in warm, sunny weather. Oh well.

Swifts are sociable birds and tend to fly in groups, wheeling around rooftops screaming or making long sweeps of the sky, often very high up. Anything up to about 15 birds may gather in one sweeping movement, and the members of the 'squadron' sometimes fly in formation, like fighter jets. The mutual screaming and wheeling – something Swallows and House Martins don't do, by the way – is a display undertaken to engender a sense of togetherness between the members of the colony, a bit like a political rally. It happens particularly often in May and June, early in the breeding season. Where Swifts scream, the nest sites cannot be far away.

Night Flights

Swifts take the airborne lifestyle to its extreme. They breed on ledges in tall buildings, but otherwise do everything on the wing, including courtship, feeding, preening and bathing. At times they also sleep while flying, and although you cannot observe them actually doing this, you can tune into the Swifts' bedtime routine.

In order to sleep aloft, a Swift must first gain altitude to at least 1,000–2,000 metres (3,280–6,560 feet). Here, it will fly into the wind, and during the course of the night it will get the dozes that it needs without fear of falling to the ground (usually fatal for a Swift, since it cannot take off again). (One may conclude, then, that Swifts don't drift into deep sleep and lose control of their basic flying ability.) At the end of a summer day, they rise high into the sky, screaming as they spiral upwards, first clearly visible, then becoming pin-pricks as the light fades. Finally, they are out of sight and their screams become distant whispers. The land darkens, and the Swifts circle in the cool night air.

ABOVE: *Groups of Swifts often fly around the rooftops, screaming.* **LEFT:** *On warm nights Swifts disappear high into the sky to sleep.*

Green Woodpecker

Although Green Woodpeckers are quite common, they are somewhat reluctant visitors to gardens. This is because they feed on the ground and feel vulnerable unless they can see danger approaching from a long way off. The small lawns and high fences of modern suburbia are not ideal. Furthermore, Green Woodpeckers also require large and often old trees for their nest-sites, so well-established, spread-out neighbourhoods are best for them.

However, if your lawn is big enough, Green Woodpeckers will pay a visit, and they are unusual among garden birds in habitually staying put in one spot while feeding, sometimes for an hour or more. Their staple food is ants, and while on the ground they make cone-shaped holes in the turf, excavated especially to cut through an ants' nest. They then wait for the ants to come out through passageways, or, once disturbed, to stream out frantically as if in response to a fire alarm. The woodpeckers can then lap them up with their long, saliva-drenched tongue.

ABOVE: *A Green Woodpecker digging in the snow to find ants in winter. They have been known to tunnel down through as much as 1m to get to their beloved food source.* BELOW LEFT: *A Great Spotted Woodpecker shows off its clinging skills.*

Great Spotted Woodpecker

We are all familiar with woodpeckers and the way in which they live and feed. For more details of the latter, refer to the section on looking after the birds in your garden (pages 147–8).

If woodpeckers are familiar visitors to your hanging bird feeders, you might be delighted in June or July to see them bringing along their young to give them a tutorial about how to find food. If you have seen this happen, you might have noticed that only one adult accompanies the juveniles on such a trip. This is because male and female woodpeckers practise 'brood-splitting', where each adult receives 'custody' of one or more young when they leave the nest, becoming entirely responsible for the welfare of its allocated offspring until they are independent. This split marks the end of woodpecker family life for the season, and henceforth the adults greet each other with detached cordiality.

Swallow

This elegant, effervescent species often nests in barns, outhouses and garages, so if your garden is semi-rural and you can offer such accommodation, you should be able to observe plenty of interesting behaviour – but please keep a respectful distance, of course. If Swallows do not nest nearby, you might see them flying around and catching insects, but that is about it, at least until the autumn.

A Swallow nest is made from mud, intermixed with items such as straw or feathers that enable the nest to expand or contract according to conditions. The adults obtain the mud by coming to the ground and scooping it up from the edges of puddles or ponds, but the rest of the ingredients they obtain by snatching them in mid-air. Swallows twisting in flight to grab straw floating in the wind is an engaging sight indeed.

Swallows also drink on the wing, flying right down to the surface and scooping water with their bills. If they need to bathe, they simply fly a little lower, splashing their tummies into the water and shaking off the excess as they gain height.

Wires and Wherefores

When the young Swallows have fledged they are brought out into the world and, as often as not, find themselves on wires, either overhead wires or low down on fences; wires obviously make convenient feeding stations, since Swallows do not feed their young on the wing. The young sit there, both bored and expectant at the same time, and greet their parent providers with a shiver of the wings and an open-mouthed plead. The parent delivers and flies off on another feeding trip, no doubt dreaming of the day when its young are independent.

That time won't be far off. In August and September, all of the young Swallows and most of the adults (a few will still be breeding), set off on a tour of Britain, gradually advancing south in a long introductory stage to their migration. This is the time when you see these birds in flocks, perched on their beloved wires or even on thorn trees, chattering excitedly and making brief sallies into the air, as if limbering up for their great journey.

ABOVE: *Swallows often nest on rafters inside barns and garages.* LEFT: *Male Swallows often sit on wires and sing.*

An Eye for the Straight (and Long) Guy

Surprising though it may seem, we are capable of telling how 'sexy' a male Swallow is. That is because scientists have shown that female Swallows preferentially select individuals with two main characteristics: first, a long tail; and second, a symmetrical tail, with both streamers of the same length.

If you look closely at the Swallows in your garden, it should be possible to grade them according to how attractive they are to potential partners. A male with an asymmetrical tail is one streamer short of being desirable, and its lot is a tough one. Its mate will almost certainly look around for opportunities to copulate with a more desirable neighbour (or several). As a result, the asymmetrical male may end up raising nestlings that are not its own. It will also receive less sneaky offers 'on the side' from other females.

In contrast, a magnificent specimen with a gorgeous, long and perfectly formed tail will be thoroughly sought after by all of its neighbours. But ladies beware. A perfect ten with a perfect tail does not a good provider make, and these testosterone-charged males may be lazy when it comes to feeding the chicks. Mind you, if an asymmetrical male gets suspicious and thinks that some of the genetic material in its nest may belong to another male, it may slacken off with the feeding, too. It looks like female Swallows cannot win this one.

ABOVE RIGHT: *A non-symmetrical tail is not very sexy.* **BELOW:** *A juvenile Swallow waits to be fed.*

House Martin

These smart birds dressed in morning suits are even easier to observe than Swallows, since they build their mud nests under the eaves of buildings rather than inside them. They are also more strictly colonial than Swallows, so you can watch the comings and goings – and interactions – of the colony members at leisure and with little fear of disturbing them.

The House Martin's nest is remarkable, not least because it does not rest upon anything in particular. A Swallow judiciously places its nest on a beam or a rafter, for example, but the House Martin's nest is simply stuck to the wall, with only its adhesive properties to hold it together under the eaves. Like a Swallow's nest, it is composed of mud pellets (between 700–1,500 of them), with some strands of plant fibre for strengthening. It is then lined with feathers, especially white ones (perhaps they absorb less heat), and left to its own devices.

When nest-building, House Martins collect mud from puddles and stream-sides, as Swallows do. These are not amateur builders gathering materials from a DIY shop, more in hope than expectation. They know exactly how much they need and what properties it must have; only mud of a certain moisture content is taken, and this, as every landscape gardener knows, is related to soil type. House Martins go to the trade section, so to speak, and get exactly what they need.

Pied Wagtail

Not for nothing is a wagtail called a wagtail, since these birds do indeed wag their tails incessantly. Fascinatingly, no scientist has yet come up with a definitive explanation as to why they do it. There's a mystery waiting to be uncovered on your garden lawn.

For most of the year, these birds are insectivorous and they catch their food in three main ways: picking it off the ground; spotting it from a distance and running to catch it; and leaping into the air on a short aerial sally. If you have nothing better to do one summer afternoon, try to record each occasion that the bird uses each method, and see which comes out on top.

ABOVE: *The cup-shaped nest of the House Martin is as distinctive as the bird itself.* **LEFT:** *A Pied Wagtail feeds by the waterside.*

Wren

As I mentioned in the last chapter, the Wren is quite a difficult bird to observe, partly because of its size and partly because it remains hidden among thick, tangled undergrowth and rarely ventures into the open. If you do see one, you'll often notice it curtseying – bobbing up and down on its perch. It does this for two possible reasons, either to make itself more conspicuous to another bird, or to help it look up and down at you (or another equally suspicious object) and thus judge how far away you are.

RIGHT: *A Wren can disappear into the tangle of undergrowth for hours on end.*
BELOW: *A Dunnock 'wing-waving'.*

Dunnock

This small brown bird with its bustling, nervous demeanour has become something of a celebrity in recent years because of its sex life. Males and females are both inclined to take more than one partner, and sometimes this means sharing spouses with rivals. Add a big clash in motivation between the sexes, and fierce rivalry between opposing males, and you have the ingredients of a colourful garden soap opera, enacted within the herbaceous border or rockery. It is just a pity that, even if you are a dedicated and thorough garden watcher, you won't be able to witness much of the unfolding drama.

You can, though, easily see one rather engaging display early in the season. It is known as wing-waving, and is exactly that; it is distinct from the Dunnock's nervous twitch of the wings in that just one wing is waved. The wave is directed at a rival male Dunnock, and is basically a threat signal to tell any interloper to disappear.

Robin

Sad is the garden without a Robin. This perky creature is the sort that leads you into its world and performs all sorts of meaningful behaviour on the stage of your lawn, flowerbed or spade. The Robin's charisma has won over countless sub-urban hearts, and helped the garden bird industry to boom. We all love it. Funny that, because in character the Robin is actually a rather charmless creature, full of hot temper and ego. It is territorial to a tee, and on occasion murderously violent. But we forgive it everything.

You will not see a cock Robin actually kill a cock Robin – although it does happen occasionally – but you are likely to see plenty of threats and posturing. Robins are endlessly confrontational. In essence, their orange-red breast is a rude slogan, a T-shirt with 'Buzz Off' firmly and permanently emblazoned upon it. When the breast is shown full-face to a rival, is it the equivalent of our two-fingered gesture. So, when two Robins are engaged in a neighbourly dispute, they first exchange blasts of song (one sings, the other responds, and so on) and then, if nothing is resolved, each manoeuvres to expose as much

of their chest to the other one as possible. For example, if one bird is above another, the top bird will lean over slightly on its perch, and the bottom bird will puff out its chest and look vertically upwards. Disputes are usually settled in this way, but fights do break out between intransigent birds, and they can last for hours.

Incidentally, a Robin in autumn may be so over-come by the red mist of aggression that its senses may desert it, and it might begin to attack its own reflection in the window, or even a car mirror. Before you come to the conclusion that such a bird is monumentally thick, just recall the silly things you have done in the name of anger, power or lust.

Robin disputes are all about territory, mainly because the species' feeding technique requires both space and peace for smooth operation. A Robin needs to be able to look down from a perch at moderate height, scanning the ground below for the movement of insects or other tasty morsels, which it can then ambush and pick up. For this to be successful, it is important that no other bird hops aimlessly into its patch and causes the insects to flee below ground, or distracts the terri-tory holder. So Robins guard their space jealously.

This perch-and-pounce feeding method requires a low perch, and this is why Robins are so keen on spades. A suitable implement placed into the earth at the end of a gardening session is, to a Robin, effectively a space laid at a dinner table. Not only is the spade an ideal vantage point, it also overlooks soil that is newly turned over: an absolute gift.

As many garden watchers know to their delight, Robins are more confiding than most other birds, readily approaching gardeners and even coming to the hand to obtain mealworms and other choice foods. This behaviour is probably derived from the Robin's habit of following large grazing mammals through forests, snapping up the inver-tebrates flushed by the disturbance of their feet.

LEFT: *Robins sit on spades for a reason – they make perfect look-out perches.* **OPPOSITE TOP LEFT:** *A Blackbird sunning – and evidently enjoying it!* **OPPOSITE TOP RIGHT:** *Two male Blackbirds confront each other in a dispute over territory.* **OPPOSITE BOTTOM:** *With a quick pull, a morsel is removed from the soil.*

Blackbird

If you have a lawn you are pretty certain to have Blackbirds using it. Indeed, they seem to consider your presence in the garden as a tiresome disturbance, and the moment you go back inside they will be down again, like overenthusiastic cleaners at the end of an office day. But if you have just mown the lawn, it's tempting to imagine them casting some grudging gratitude your way as they resume feeding.

Blackbirds hunt in a particular way that is easy to watch. They move across the lawn in stop-start fashion, interspersing little runs or hops of a metre or two with intense scans over the surface of the grass. They often follow a straight line, and, if things are looking unproductive in one direction, they will simply turn and go off on another tangent. If their search reveals something edible – an earthworm surfacing, for example – they will run forwards and grab it, pulling it out with some effort. And so they cover the lawn's surface with a certain thoroughness.

Blackbirds also feed in leaf litter, tossing aside surface debris with a disdainful flick of the bill, at the same time often scratching backwards with their feet to dig in a bit. This usually uncovers something to eat. When Blackbirds forage in this way they can make a loud rustling noise, which can be quite scary if you are unaware what is in the bushes. In autumn and winter, Blackbirds also eat berries in large quantities, taking them straight off the bushes.

By early spring, Blackbirds begin to exert their influence over your garden, especially if they are the territory holders. The main territorial defence is singing, but they also confront challengers by a ruffling of the feathers and a spreading of the tail. Fighting is quite common and involves birds essentially facing up to each other and meeting head-on, bill and claws furiously pecking and scrabbling. The combatants often flutter a metre or so into the air. Fights are usually resolved

quickly, but deaths have been recorded. Both sexes will defend the territory with posturing and aggression, although serious confrontations are usually between members of the same sex.

In summer, you may see Blackbirds sunbathing on the lawn or in a flowerbed. It is a popular activity, which the birds seem to 'enjoy'; it may warm them up in the morning, help to remove parasites and get their feathers in better order. A sunbathing bird may look like it is injured. It 'lies' on the ground with wings and tail spread and the rest of the feathers ruffled; at the same time, it may pant with bill open. In fact, if anything, it is feeling ecstatic.

Song Thrush

The Song Thrush has a talent that no other bird in the garden possesses, which is to smash snails against a hard surface so that the shell breaks open and the edible body is exposed.

This may not sound earth-shattering, but if you consider that to a bird a snail is quite heavy, and that the Song Thrush has only its bill to work with, then you can perhaps appreciate the feat a little more. And there is a real knack to the procedure. The bird doesn't just throw the snail against the rock or ground, but keeps hold of it, dashing it against the hard surface with a combined downward movement and sideways turn of the head. Like any good craftsman, the Song Thrush requires

the right tools. The hard surface, known as the anvil, must be in an easily accessible place so that the thrush can approach at the correct angle, and at the right height. Within the garden certain anvils become favourites, and these sites are littered with the fragments of broken shells.

Another property that must also be of importance to the thrush is how much noise the anvil makes. It always requires a series of hits to break the shell open, and that may be time enough for a Blackbird to hear the beats and hurry down to steal the Song Thrush's hard-earned meal. The Blackbird does not have the ability to break open snail shells, but it is quick to take advantage of those that can.

Song Thrushes feed in a similar way to Blackbirds and on many of the same foods – earthworms from the lawn, insects from leaf litter, fruit from trees. Like Blackbirds, they often cock their head to one side when standing still, as if listening to sounds from the ground below. In fact, that's exactly what they are doing. At intervals they suddenly leap into action, digging down into a particular piece of soil like treasure-hunters with a bleeping metal-detector, until they find what they have heard, often grubs moving about in the subsurface soil.

BELOW LEFT: *The Song Thrush listens for prey under the surface.* **BELOW:** *The Song Thrush is the only garden bird that can smash open snail shells.*

Mistle Thrush

The main activity you are likely to see from the Mistle Thrush is some form of aggressive behaviour. These are the largest thrushes and use their bulk to protect what is theirs, either the nest during the breeding season or a long-lasting supply of berries in the winter.

The winter activity is particularly interesting and if you have a holly tree in the garden you might just see it in action. Mistle Thrushes, working as individuals or pairs, effectively requisition the tree and its berries for their sole personal use from October until the following spring. They feed from it only sparingly most of the time, concentrating on ground-feeding instead if the weather is mild, but that does not stop them excluding other birds with fierce and noisy attacks. Their aim is to keep berry supplies in stock as an insurance against harsh weather and shortages of other foods. The holly tree is thus a living larder, a savings account for a rainy day.

ABOVE: *A Spotted Flycatcher turns its skills to plucking autumn berries.* **BELOW LEFT:** *When hunting, a Spotted Flycatcher typically dashes out from a perch, snaps up an insect, and returns to the same perch again.*

Spotted Flycatcher

It is easy to see a Spotted Flycatcher feeding as it leaps from its perch to snap at flying insects; that is its profession, so to speak, and if you have flycatchers in your garden you will see them doing this all the time. Birds usually have favourite feeding – or launching – perches in their territory, and if you have a little spare time to watch, you could map these and see which is used most often.

If it rains or is windy, Spotted Flycatchers are forced to abandon their usual aerial sallies, as these are bound to be unproductive; the birds are effectively grounded. At such times they take insects straight from the leaves, and occasionally feed on the ground.

When feeding young, the adults keep themselves going by eating the smaller insects that they catch. If they snap up something large and juicy, such as a bluebottle, it will be delivered to the nest and the hungry young.

Long-tailed Tit

The engaging Long-tailed Tit has so much charisma that when visiting gardens it tends to grab the attention and is easily watched. The first and most obvious thing you will notice is that it is almost invariably seen in flocks (except in the breeding season between late February and May). A flock of Long-tailed Tits is clearly a unit, the birds following each other through the garden one by one, each taking care not to be left behind.

These flocks, which move restlessly from garden to garden, forever moving on, are rather special. In contrast to those of other species, which tend to be made up of unrelated strangers, Long-tailed Tit groups are gatherings of close relatives. In early autumn, a typical flock will consist of an adult pair, up to eight of their offspring from the most recent breeding season, plus some uncles and aunts from the male's side. Later on in the winter, the female young leave the flock to prevent inbreeding, and are replaced by unrelated partners for the flock's young males.

At night these birds huddle together for warmth, all in a line on a perch. Huddling is an unusual activity among birds, which tend to abhor close bodily contact with others and instead seek personal space like passengers on commuter train. But Long-tailed Tits cannot survive cold winter nights without it.

Even if you have a regular flock, you are unlikely to come across the birds huddling at night. You might, though, be fortunate enough to see juveniles 'cuddling' in the summer, since they often do so by day. If you can hear a Long-tailed Tit kefuffle from late May to July and the birds appear to be going nowhere fast, then there may be some young gathered on a perch deep in the tree or bush, feathers touching.

The other behaviour you might be able to witness, if these birds breed nearby, is a pair collecting nest material. Most species of bird construct their nests with considerable haste and minimal rigour, like typical corporate house-builders, but Long-tailed Tits spend up to three weeks in late February and March collecting thousands of items for their incredibly intricate structures. They use four main ingredients, including moss, lichens and cobwebs, but you are most likely to see them carrying feathers, of which they collect many hundreds. Watch for this activity on sunny mornings.

LEFT: *A brood of juvenile Long-tailed Tits will often perch cuddled close together.* **OPPOSITE:** *A Blue Tit on its short, whirring song-flight.*

Blue Tit

The Blue Tit is such a common bird that it is easy to overlook its qualities – not only its glorious colouration (who said British birds were dull?) but also its inquisitive, perky behaviour. Blue Tits have often forced themselves into our consciousness by adopting unusual feeding methods that have interfered with the house-hold; for example, pecking putty from edges of windows and drinking from the tops of milk bottles. So this is the sort of bird that, at times, will simply make you watch it.

In spring, look out for a courtship display. If you have a nest-box in your garden, you might see a pair visiting it very early on in the season, in January or February. The visitors may fly in and perch at the entrance mysteriously pecking around the edges, apparently measuring up the hole to check the box's poten-tial as a nest-site. Effectively this is what they are doing, although they will not begin breeding in earnest until April.

At about the same time of year, you might witness a display flight. This is a subtle piece of behaviour, consisting of a bird flying on a horizontal route between one perch and another. The only thing that draws the attention is that the flight does not seem quite 'right': it is too slow, and the birds may be flapping overfast, or alternatively, slowly like a butterfly. This display flight often ends close to a potential nest-site, a property than the couple are considering for the raising of their young.

Owing to this species' habit of nesting in boxes, it is relatively easy to enjoy the intimacies of Blue Tit family life. You could always buy one of those videocam nest-boxes and watch the drama, but it is a lot cheaper just to watch from outside. Look out in particular for the male feeding the female while the latter is incubating the eggs. Known as courtship-feeding (our version is taking a girl out to dinner), it is a way for the male to provision the female while most of her energies are put into

caring for the young. Although the incubating bird will take regular breaks to feed herself, these extra food parcels brought in by the male are vital for her welfare.

Once the eggs have hatched – and there may be as many as 18 of them – every garden watcher can sympathize with the adults' subsequent treadmill of finding a caterpillar, flying to the nest, delivering it to a begging chick, flying out again, finding another caterpillar, flying back to the nest, and so on, again and again. It is well-known that, between them, the two parent Blue Tits may make 1,000 visits a day to keep their young provisioned, which must be an exhausting task. For us, watching in delight, it's a bit like sitting back and following a marathon on TV, admiring the athletes' display of guts and endurance while adhering firmly to our armchairs.

It is easier to see tits bringing in food than perhaps any other group of birds. They make more visits than most and bring quite large, highly visible food items, carrying them in the bill. If you have ever wondered why they don't simply collect lots of caterpillars in one go and feed several young at a time, it appears that the adults need to process each prey item en route to the nest, breaking the jaws of the leaf-muncher before entrusting it to the frail mouths of the young.

Great Tit

It is not really a question of survival of the fattest, but the Great Tit – the largest and plumpest member of the tit family – certainly does occupy the top of the hierarchy among these nimble birds. When three or more species are competing at a hanging bird feeder, the Great Tit will usually hold sway over Blue, Marsh and Coal Tits, using aggression and threats to keep its feet firmly on the wire mesh. However, it must not put on too much fat in its position as 'chief executive' because an overfed Great Tit is an easier and slower target for a garden Sparrowhawk.

In early spring, a Great Tit's aggression often turns towards members of its own species, since this is the time that the males lay

claim to territories for their own exclusive use. Their main technique to establish a territory is singing, but when two males confront each other face to face, they adopt a special fluffed-out, upright posture designed to show off their black breast stripe to best effect.

The females are attracted by the song and will in fact refrain from showing any interest in a male unless he has a territory to defend. Pairs are formed from January onwards, and from then on the males make short song-flights directed towards the nest-hole, in the same manner as a Blue Tit.

ABOVE: *A Great Tit sings upon its perch, notifying rivals that he is the owner of the territory.* **LEFT:** *A Great Tit takes a nut that has been thoughtfully wedged into the tree bark.* **OPPOSITE TOP:** *A Coal Tit grabs a nut and spirits away before it can be stolen.*

Coal Tit

As the smallest tit in the garden, the Coal Tit always has to watch its step. It is constantly under threat of bullying by Blue and Great Tits, which steal its food and prevent it getting ready access to food sources, including the bird table. The larger, more colourful tits run a totalitarian regime and the Coal Tit is one of their subjects!

However, the Coal Tit does have one trick to keep its head above water and prevent it from starving, and if you have Coal Tits visiting your feeders you will have seen it in action. Notice how, when a Coal Tit visits, it zooms in, grabs a nut or seed, and then dashes away again before it can be attacked, almost like a nervous person using an inner-city cash dispensing machine. It usually returns very soon afterwards and goes through the same routine again. Between these quick-fire visits, the Coal Tit goes away to a dense-leafed tree such as a conifer. Looking around to make sure that no-one is watching, it then hides the food away in between the needles, or in the bark, or even on the ground. It will continue storing food and then, later, it will wait for a quiet moment before it revisits its hidden cache to eat at its leisure.

Scoring Skirmishes

There is no better place to watch birds in direct competition than a bird table or hanging feeder. A reliable food source is like gold dust to any bird, and it is inevitable that they fight over it. Some birds are prevented from entering the fray and others are barged from the scene the moment that they arrive.

For this project, the idea is to record the outcome of aggressive encounters. The encounters will not be fights as such, but usually pecks, hops and flights in an effort to displace a competitor. A few minutes of observation will soon establish the sorts of aggressive encounters birds enter into. Each time one bird attacks or displaces another, record the two species involved (not just tits, but all others, too) and also note the outcome. So, if a Blue Tit displaces a Coal Tit you could record it as BT–CT, and if one Blue Tit displaces another you could record that as BT–BT; if multiple displacements occur, record these as, say, GT–3BT. After a while, you will soon establish the hierarchy at your feeder in regard to species. If you begin to recognize certain individuals, you can log even more information.

Gradually, you can record the situation under different conditions, and answer such questions as: is there more aggression in the morning and evening than at other times of day? Do outcomes change during the day, or in different weather or seasons? Is one sex dominant over another? Scoring skirmishes will be fun and will enable you to uncover a wealth of information.

Nuthatch

The name 'Nuthatch' has arisen from the words 'nut' and 'hack', referring to the way in which Nuthatches wedge nuts or fruit in fissures of bark and hammer them open. The sound they make while doing this is quite similar to the pecking of a foraging woodpecker, and, in the same way, the bird absolutely throws itself at the recalcitrant nut, leaning its head well back between each hammer blow. This is an easy behaviour to see and hear, often taking place not far from a well-stocked bird table, as well as up in the branches of a mature tree. Watching a bird at work, slamming its bill forward, it is hard to see how it manages to hold on with its feet.

The answer, in fact, is that Nuthatches have sharp claws and very big feet – equivalent to at least a size 40 in our measurement system! This foot power enables them to creep up, down and around tree bark, often very rapidly. Their descents are particularly unusual because

ABOVE: *A Jay carries off an acorn to store away.*
BELOW LEFT: *The Nuthatch commonly wedges nuts into the bark so that it can hack them open.*

they are the only 'creeping' birds to be able to climb downwards head first. They do it, essentially, by momentarily hanging down from one foot (like a bat), while the other gains a hold further down, so whenever they are on a trunk the feet are held wide apart.

If you have Nuthatches in the garden, they will be particularly active in autumn. This is when they collect large quantities of nuts to store away in their territory, mainly in the bark well above ground. In spring, Nuthatches breed in holes in trees or in nest-boxes. Since these are always in short supply and there is much competition from other species, especially Starlings, Nuthatches make a very distinctive modification to their accommodation: a coating of mud. The mud is plastered all over the nest-site by the female, inside and out, and it is concentrated at the entrance to narrow the way in. Effectively, the Nuthatch bricks up the sides of the hole to prevent larger birds from gaining access. Smaller competitors are repulsed by a few threatened stabs from the Nuthatch's dagger-like bill.

Jay

Jays are usually found in leafy, quiet neighbour-hoods with plenty of large trees, and here the birds tend to live a secretive life up in the canopy, where they are not easy to observe. All this changes in October and November, when Jays must visit the avian equivalent of out-of-town retail centres in order to collect food for the coming winter.

The food concerned is acorns. Acorns are hard-shelled, long-lasting nuts that are ideal for a winter food store, but they must, of course, be collected and taken away from oak trees. For Jays living in territories without oaks, this involves countless treks to and from their nearest outlet to collect the nuts, three to nine at a time, and these commuting journeys are the reason why Jays are far easier to see in autumn than at any other time of the year.

The acorns are stored away, one at a time, either in the ground or under leaf litter. Where a Jay's territory encompasses a garden, this painstaking concealing process is reasonably easy to observe.

Magpie

As every bird gardener knows, where Magpies occur they are easy to see and hear. They rarely get away with their well-known breeding season raids on the eggs and nests of smaller birds, such as Blackbirds, Song Thrushes, Robins and Chaffinches – tits, which nest in holes, are rarely harassed – so their danger to garden birds is dis-proportionately exaggerated. Nevertheless, they do make quite a song and dance of their summer taste for meat, attacking in broad daylight and causing noisy alarm calls from their enraged vic-tims. The chances are that, if a Magpie indiscre-tion occurs while you are awake and in the house, your attention will probably be drawn to it.

The birds often attack in pairs, either using plain violence or being more strategic, with, for example, one bird causing a distraction while the other steals into the unguarded nest. With their size advantage, superior 'intelligence' and evi-dently thorough knowledge of the garden's small birds, Magpies appear to be ruthless killers of the weak. But, in reality, they are nothing more than successful opportunists.

It is easy to see Magpies when they perch at the top of trees and that, indeed, is the birds' intention – to be seen. These crows have no territorial song as such, so the practice of 'Treetop Sitting', as it's officially termed, is their way of claiming tacit possession, like the proverbial tourist guarding a deckchair.

Most Magpies live in pairs in a fixed territory, but there are never enough of these to go round to satisfy demand. So at certain times the leaders of the local gang of disenfranchised or displaced young Magpies make an audacious bid for a patch of ground by plonking themselves within an occupied territory and picking a fight with the incumbents. They rarely win, but they create quite a storm. In the ensuing conflict all the local Magpies, both paired and unpaired, collect to watch the fight, like people on a crowded street at pub turning-out time. There is much noise and excitement, and, if it happens in your garden, you simply cannot miss it.

BELOW: *It may not be obvious what it's doing, but this Magpie is displaying its presence in its territory.*

Rook

If you live within sight or sound of a Rookery, you won't have much difficulty observing plenty of wholesome and unwholesome behaviour. Being colonial, Rooks' lives – their conflicts, relationships, triumphs and disasters – are led in the public eye.

At the nests, you will see plenty of robbery, especially in January and February. Rook constructions are refurbished if not rebuilt every year, exposed as they are to destructive treetop weather, and this, of course, requires materials. The effort of undertaking a stick-breaking trip is much weightier and more tiresome than a quick jaunt to an adjoining tree, so the birds readily steal from their neighbours. Many males also attempt to rape incubating females that are not their own mates. These intrusions are rarely successful, but an incident provokes much disapproval, with exaggerated bowing, scuffling and guttural caws.

The sure sign that a male and female Rook are officially an 'item' is when the male feeds the female beak to beak; copulation may follow. Don't confuse this with an adult bird feeding a youngster. The wing-shivering and pleading of the recipient is the same, but the time of year at which it takes place, from autumn (when most pairs are formed) until about March, is not.

Rooks breed early in the year to ensure that they can find plenty of earthworms for the growing young before the ground dries out in warmer weather. The first eggs are laid in late March. In just over two weeks they hatch, and the sexes divide their roles. The female remains on the nest, while the male searches for food for the family, bringing it back at regular intervals in his crop, which appears visibly distended and bulbous as he flies in. In April, therefore, almost every Rook flying to and fro between a colony and nearby fields will be a male.

RIGHT: *Rooks pair for life.*

Carrion Crow

We may not appreciate dustmen as much as they deserve, but we do miss them when they don't turn up to collect our refuse. In the same way, we do not naturally warm to the Carrion Crow. However, in common with several equally unpopular birds such as gulls and Magpies, it provides a useful service by putting its bill where we would fear to tread. Not for nothing is it called the Carrion Crow, and many road-kills of small mammals and birds, plus various other unsavoury items, find their way into Carrion Crows' stomachs. It is the vulture syndrome: useful but unloved, ugly but essential.

Carrion Crows are very much omnivores, and this, combined with their opportunism and 'intelligence', means that they are always interesting to watch, if you can bear to do it. They do, for example, often take bread and other items from bird tables and dunk them in the water before swallow-

ing, presumably knowing that dried bread could be harmful to them. They also regularly store food away in hidey holes for a short time, to be retrieved when required (although much of it is perishable and so will not last long).

For food-storing to be useful, the hoarding bird must of course remember where it hid the cache, and crows most definitely have the mental facilities to do this. In fact, they also use their memory to find the nests of birds in spring and summer, so that they can subsequently feed on the eggs and young. They do not necessarily remember the exact spot – and, anyway, the smaller birds may not use precisely the same site again – but they gain an idea in their mind's eye of potentially productive places in which to look: a mental 'search image'.

Carrion Crows, in contrast to Rooks, always nest in their own territory, well away from other pairs, never in colonies; one way to remember this is that a ship has only one crow's nest. The species' intricate, lovingly-built nest is one of the few bird nests placed near the top of a tree. Thanks to this lofty vantage point, Carrion Crows are often first on the scene in defending the area from predators, and can often be seen up in the sky harassing Kestrels, Sparrowhawks, broad-winged Grey Herons and other real or imagined dangerous species. Any Carrion Crow croak from high in the sky should always engender an upward glance from a hopeful birdwatcher.

ABOVE LEFT: *Living up to its name...* **ABOVE:** *In Scotland or Ireland the all black Carrion Crow is replaced by the smart two-coloured Hooded Crow.* **BELOW:** *Crow dunking bread into a bird bath.*

Jackdaw

Following the memorable definition given in Helen Fielding's *Bridget Jones's Diary*, Jackdaws are the epitome of 'Smug Marrieds': couples always together, overtly affectionate and delivering an ever-present slap in the face to frustrated singles. Indeed, few birds are so dedicated to being part of a pair, regularly remaining together even after an unsuccessful breeding attempt, which is almost unheard of among birds generally. Jackdaws usually breed in large colonies, and whenever the members of a colony take to the sky, which they often do, the flock can still be made out as a conglomeration of twosomes.

When not flying, Jackdaws smooch in two main ways: they cuddle together to preen one another; and the male brings food offerings to the female, and feeds her bill to bill when she begs. These are the signs of an established pair, which can be seen at any time of year.

The Jackdaw is literally tarred with the same black brush as the other species of crow, but it is much less predatory, at least on vertebrates, and does not scavenge very much. It is most at home on fields and long pasture, especially in sheep-rearing country, and it actually eats more invertebrates

than anything else. It does visit lawns, but can be extremely wary of close contact with people. One of the most obvious pieces of behaviour shown by Jackdaws is their aerial manoeuvring. All of the birds in a colony, or members of several colonies sharing a roost, often fly up into the air with no apparent warning to indulge in aerobatics of various kinds. The Jackdaws soar, tumble and turn, all to a cacophonous accompaniment. It can be quite a sight and sound, especially when performed, as it frequently is, against the backdrop of a setting sun.

ABOVE: *On the ground Jackdaws have a characteristic jaunty walk.*
LEFT: *A Jackdaw colony performs aerial manoeuvres at sunset.*
OPPOSITE TOP: *The Cuckoo at the bottom of the garden? A female Starling awaits her moment (top), then steals in and dumps an egg in her neighbour's nest.* **OPPOSITE BOTTOM:** *At dusk Starlings gather together prior to roosting.*

Starling

You wouldn't want a Starling as a dinner guest. When these birds arrive on bird tables or lawns in gangs, they have the habit of greedily gobbling up their food as fast as they possibly can, like the workhouse boys in Oliver Twist. But much as this habit looks revolting, it is an adaptation to ensuring that they are in a vulnerable position (i.e. out in the open) for as short a time as possible.

Starlings on the lawn are a common sight, but they have an uncommon method of foraging. A good many birds take food straight from the lawn's surface, and some, including the Blackbird and Mistle Thrush, may actually dig into the lawn, but none do it quite like a Starling. It has very powerful muscles that open its bill (we, in contrast, have strong muscles to shut our mouth). And so, by inserting its bill into the soil and then opening it, it creates a little hole; as the bird probes in again, its eyes swivel forward to help it judge distance. Thus, it can spot clues in its search for insect larvae such as those of craneflies, or daddy-long-legs.

Starlings nest in holes, and, where possible, they do so socially, perhaps on trees or guttering. The males are easy to see in late winter and early spring, singing outside their holes, often several at once. Starlings have some interesting breeding habits, such as the unusual practice of laying extra eggs in the nests of neighbours. This is known as

egg-dumping; you will not see it in action. The brownish young are chucked out of the territory a few days after fledging and forced to fend for themselves. In June and July, they form large flocks and can be seen on lawns and other productive feeding sites. The adults join them later in the autumn.

Starlings are also renowned for their communal roosts, which can include many thousands of birds. They gather in the evening and rest on buildings, as well as in reedbeds and scrub in the surrounding countryside. Although you won't see anything spectacular from most gardens, you can often see flocks of these birds making a bee-line over your house in the evening to the town centre or other roosting site; ironically, they are commuting into the conurbation as the human workers are crowding the outbound routes on their journey home.

House Sparrow

The House Sparrow was once so common that to take an interest in it would have been considered somewhat demeaning to someone with a mind for enquiry. Nowadays, with the species' numbers declining, House Sparrow watching and counting has become acceptable, even trendy.

And so it should be. The House Sparrow is an engaging bird with a lively social life, and, if you are in an area with sparrows, it is easy to observe. One of its overlooked features is also one of the most remarkable – its extraordinary dependence on humans, their affairs and their buildings. You simply don't get House Sparrows in wild places, and that's pretty unusual.

These birds live in colonies, and you should be able to attest to that fact in your garden easily enough. The birds are forever gathering together to make cheeping noises, which can be conversational or deafening,

like a group of teenagers at a loose end. In fact, members of a colony show great solidarity and do most of the things in life – nesting, preening, feeding – together.

One type of sparrow behaviour that is easily observed, especially in summer, is dust-bathing. The term sums it up. The birds find a spot of dry earth and bathe there in exactly the same way as they would – and do – immerse themselves in water. It is thought that this form of behaviour helps to remove parasites and surplus preen-oil from the plumage, and, watching sparrows revel in it, it is hard to escape the conclusion that it must be enjoyable.

Look out too for other cameos of interesting behaviour. On some summer days, for example, when flying ants swarm, House Sparrows try their hand at catching them in flight, making aerial sallies like overweight flycatchers, and being surprisingly successful. At other times they will use their flying ability to take off suddenly in pursuit of pigeons that are flapping harmlessly by, for reasons that are still obscure. They also eat crocuses and will try out most food put out intentionally in the garden.

A House Sparrow nest is a real cheap affair, a bit of straw thrown together with little apparent cohesion and craft. The sparrows fly in and out, delivering material like builders desperate to get the job done as soon as possible.

Chaffinch

If Chaffinches are a year-long feature of your garden, you might have noticed something that sets them apart from other members of the family: their sociability, or lack of it. They gather together in flocks in winter, alright, when hundreds may join together to feed or to roost. However, in summer they are distinctly snooty. You see one on its own, or a pair, or possibly a family party. But you never see the jovial, chatty gatherings in dinner-party-sized numbers that are so typical of Greenfinches and Goldfinches.

This is because the Chaffinch feeds itself and its young on insects in the summer, and not on seeds. Insects are so abundant that a Chaffinch, in contrast to a Greenfinch or Goldfinch, can defend a private territory and keep its distance from others of its kind. Indeed, Chaffinches appear to slip into the canopy of trees when the leaves are out, and make themselves hard to spot. The members of a pair have quite a stiff, non-intimate relationship and again, in contrast to other finches, are often seen apart, whereas other finch pairs are inseparable.

OPPOSITE TOP: *A House Sparrow loafs on a perch. These birds hang around a lot, apparently not doing much.* **OPPOSITE BOTTOM:** *An unusual meal in early spring.* **BELOW:** *Alone among the finches, the Chaffinch catches many insects in flight.*

Greenfinch

Most garden watchers write the Greenfinch off as a bird-feeder bully, but it is no more aggressive than many other species. It can, though, treat a bird feeder as its own property and keep others away while it holds court for long periods of time.

In common with the Goldfinch, the Greenfinch is sociable all year long, even when breeding. You'll probably find that in the summer you will receive visits from small groups of perhaps 6–8 birds, and all of these individuals will be near neighbours to each other, living in the same 'street'. They often club together on communal foraging trips, leaving their small individual territories all at the same time and working in a team to look for food. Once they return, they will retire each to their own nests, just as human neighbours would do after a day trip.

Greenfinches also seem to sing occasionally as a team. This is because, in contrast to species such as Robins or Chaffinches, their songs are not for territorial spacing, but more to delight the female to which they are paired. If they really feel like showing off, they will take off from a high perch and perform a display flight. Flying on a level course, they describe wide circles or figures of eight, flapping slowly with exaggerated wingbeats, singing all the while. This exuberant performance is a common sight around bushy gardens from March–July.

Male Greenfinches provision their females in the spring, so if you see one bird feeding the other in the early part of the season, don't be fooled into thinking that any young have fledged just yet.

ABOVE: *Greenfinches are regular visitors to feeders, where they keep well apart.* **LEFT:** *The Greenfinch's looping song-flight.*

Siskin

You probably won't see a Siskin doing anything other than eating food; or perhaps you will – digesting food. Siskins are rather special in that they can ingest more food than their stomachs can store or process, carrying the excess in a little pocket in their gullet. If, then, you see a Siskin on a perch just singing, or even ruffling its feathers and keeping still, there may be a great deal happening in its alimentary canal.

These small finches have the curious habit of feeding while in an upside-down position. Various other birds may do this, but usually only momentarily, whereas Siskins appear to do so preferentially. So far, nobody seems to have worked out why.

When Siskins come into gardens, usually in late winter, they often do so as pairs. This is because males and females often meet up in winter flocks, and undertake the journey to their breeding sites together.

Goldfinch

The Goldfinch can give the impression of being beautiful to look at but unremarkable in character. This is partly because pretty much all it does in a garden is eat. The nest is hidden away high in a tree, and is where most of the Goldfinch's complex social and sexual displays take place. It is a fleeting, one-dimensional garden visitor.

In the autumn months, you can watch the attractive sight of adult Goldfinches feeding their fledged young. And on the feeders you might be surprised how these fragile-looking beauties can be aggressive to other birds.

ABOVE: *A Goldfinch on teasel, a favourite food plant.* **RIGHT:** *Siskins often feed upside down, but nobody seems to know quite why.*

Bullfinch

Bullfinches materialize. You don't see them coming and you don't hear them coming. Your bud-studded bush or feeder is one moment unadorned, and the next moment it plays host to a pair or party of these clean-cut lovelies. There may appear to be no middle ground.

Being somewhat elusive creatures, Bullfinches do not show you much easily observed behaviour; no exaggerated displays such as song flights, or spectacular conflicts. They are so keen on their privacy that all of the important events in their lives happen in secret. But there is one very unusual event that you might appreciate by proxy, so to speak – you cannot actually see it, but you can be sure that it is happening.

If there are Bullfinches present in your garden between April and August, when they are breeding, they will at some point need to carry food to their young. The majority of species either hold food in the bill or regurgitate it from the gullet (as with the seed-paste produced by adult Goldfinches). But Bullfinches carry plant matter in pouches, a bit like a hamster. These pouches form on either side of the bill and act like built-in shopping bags, increasing the food-carrying capacity. The pouches develop specially for the breeding season, and are lost soon afterwards.

BELOW : *Bullfinches feed their young on regurgitated plant matter than they store in pouches in the side of the mouth.* **OPPOSITE:** *Herring Gulls are usually seen flying over.*

Lovely Lists

Most people make a list of the birds they see in their garden, whether or not they admit it. In birdwatching circles, making lists is sometimes frowned upon as trivial, as if it somehow sullies one's appreciation of the birds and makes them all into 'names and numbers'.

This, of course, is nonsense and absolutely everyone should make a list of every bird species they see in the garden. It's fun to collect bird sightings, and you can be competitive about it, too, if you wish.

Make year lists, month lists, day lists, mental lists, lists written on the fridge, lists of species, lists of males and females, lists of birds you have heard, birds that feed at the table, birds that visits a certain tree, birds that you have seen courting, copulating, defecating – anything you like.

The overall list of birds you have seen in the garden is special because it can be seen as part of your house-

hold. The birds that have visited are personal, like no others, because they have shared your acreage. A list can be full of memories, and, delightfully, its gaps can also leave you full of anticipation. What will the next bird that you see and identify be?

Many garden watchers only include birds that actually visit their garden, touching down within its borders. That's fine, but I suggest that that narrows the field too much. Your list should include everything that flies over your garden as well; everything, indeed, that you can see from your house or garden. This makes good ornithological sense because it will include aerial birds such as Swifts, migratory birds flying over, and birds such as gulls or ducks that ply a daily route. It will encompass more of your neighbourhood. To include 'fly-overs' also makes you a better birdwatcher as you will learn to keep looking up.

Chapter 3

Listening to Birds

You may think that it is a bit daft to devote an entire chapter of a book to the subject of bird sounds; after all, you'll have to imagine the songs and calls as you read about them. But many sounds in the garden are more familiar than you might think. We all know the caw of a Carrion Crow, the coo of a pigeon and the cheep of a House Sparrow. They are very much part of the garden scene, and invade every birdwatcher's consciousness.

This section will give you an idea of the main sounds of our noisier featured species. The majority of descriptions should be easy to follow, and where possible I have included mnemonics – special memory aids – that will allow you as a reader to fix a sound in your head. The Dunnock's song, for example, cannot be written down on paper, but when you hear it described as sounding like the squeaky wheels of a trolley, the sound comes alive.

ABOVE: *Wren.*
OPPOSITE: *A Greenfinch uttering its rasping wheeze.*

Learning bird sounds is difficult on the whole, but the garden is blessed with some fine singers and some very distinctive bird noises. It is a good place to dip your toes into the ocean of bird vocalizations, so that you can start slowly and see if you wish to go on.

Listening to birds has an equivalent to the fast-track identification system for visual recognition described in the first chapter (see page 8). You cannot describe a sound in the same way, from bill to tail, but you can still describe it carefully. Try to put it into words (not necessarily real ones): 'tseep' will do, for example. Take note of how repetitive it is and in what context it is being made – is the bird alarmed, for example? Where is the sound coming from, and how high up? What time of day is it and what season of the year? In bird song or call recognition, all of these factors can be important.

Chapter 4 includes a calendar of important bird songs and calls.

Bird Songs and Calls

Our world would be a very dull place without communication: we would be lost if we could not talk to each other. For birds it is the same, and the 'songs' and 'calls' that we hear are full of meaning; they are a language. Through songs and calls birds can show anxiety, fear, desire, urgency, passion and frustration; they insult one another, lay themselves bare, defend their territorial borders and advertise for partners. The open air is the birds' internet, full of information and available to the public bird community at large.

Before going into any specifics, we need to get a good handle on the two broad types of sounds that birds make, since these terms will be used extensively in the sections that follow. They are:

OPPOSITE: *A gathering of Starlings at dusk makes a formidable screeching racket.* **ABOVE:** *A singing bird is almost always a male – except for the Robin.* **BELOW RIGHT.** *Small bird, big voice – the Wren punches above its weight with its noisy song.*

Calls

These are usually sounds of one or two syllables such as 'cheep' or 'tick', although some are longer, such as the panicky alarm-rattle of a Blackbird. Calls are used year-round in a variety of contexts, including alarm, flight-contact and threat. Calls are usually dictated by circumstance, so you could see them as reactive rather than proactive. A bird makes an alarm call in reaction to danger, and calls to its peers to ensure that they are still nearby.

Songs

Songs, on the other hand, are usually more elaborate utterances than calls. They are sentences, if you like, rather than simply words. They are used mainly in the breeding season, and almost exclusively by males, and have both a territorial and sexual function. By singing, a bird lays claim to a part of your garden, reserving it, as far as its own species is concerned, for itself. It is like a flag put down by a prospector to lay claim to mining rights, but it is an aural flag rather than a visual one. The singer is the bird in possession, and the song is a challenge and warning to others.

Of course, females hear these songs, too. To a female bird, a song is like a lonely hearts advertisement, proclaiming availability. A female can listen to all of the males in her neighbourhood and assess their singing ability, and this gives her an insight into each male's qualities before she even meets him. A bird's singing performance is affected by all sorts of things, including his age, experience, state of health, readiness to breed and his response to the weather. This is valuable information for the listener.

Reading the above, you will conclude two important things about songs: they are uttered mainly or exclusively in the breeding season, and each male varies its output. In fact, a particular species' repertoire varies, too: some males have better and more interesting songs than others. But fear not, although each male in theory has its own song, it also has to sing a song that is recognizably that of its species. It follows, then, that it is recognizable to us.

Advertising Calls

These are mid-way between songs and calls. They are sexually motivated like songs, but are made by birds such as pigeons and gulls, the utterances of which are not normally thought of as songs in the usual sense.

Black-headed and Herring Gulls

If you live in a seaside town you will need no introduction to the sounds of the Herring Gull. Herring Gulls are the ones that sit on nearby rooftops and belt out their clamorous utterances from dawn to dusk.

The main sequence you hear, the one beginning with some long drawn-out notes that quicken in pace, is known as the 'Long Call'. It is basically a long-distance challenge to all gulls nearby that the rooftop is occupied, and the motivation is similar to that of a politician driving through a neighbourhood speaking to constituents through a loudspeaker: power through self-advertisement.

Herring Gulls also make incessant wailing sounds, often with rather a tragic tone, and these are mostly contact calls between pairs or flock members. Another sound is a quick, laughing 'ga-ga-ga-ga', which indicates a mood of slight alarm.

Most gardeners will not hear much from the Black-headed Gull. All its calls are shriller than those of a Herring Gull, with a vibrating quality.

ABOVE: *If you've got Collared Doves, you'll know their cooing only too well.* **BELOW LEFT:** *Gulls are noisy birds. This is a first winter Black-headed Gull.*

Collared Dove

If you have Collared Doves in the garden you will probably already be familiar with their song. It consists of three notes and sounds a bit like a somewhat depressed football fan chanting 'Un-i-ted'. By contrast, the Woodpigeon's song consists of five notes, not three (see below).

Collared Doves have a habit of delivering this dirge from aerials and rooftops, to make sure the whole neighbourhood can hear it clearly. Every so often they leap into the air and perform a song flight. Upon landing they are so delighted with their efforts that they give several triumphant nasal calls – these sound rather like those children's trumpets that unroll when you blow them and tickle people's faces. For extra effect, the Collared Dove adds in a slow lift of its tail when making this call.

Incidentally, at a distance the Collared Dove's song has a very similar tone to the Cuckoo. It is probable that a lot of the very earliest spring Cuckoos reported to the newspapers are actually misheard Collared Doves – so be wary of this.

Feral Pigeon

The Feral Pigeon has a display flight that is often accompanied by a clapping of the wings. However, its most common sound is a coo that is usually heard from displaying males as they chase ever-reluctant females across the ground. If you have a group of pigeons near you, they may use your roof for display and the coos will be audible from your patio.

The coo is not easy to describe, but it is gentle and a little exclamatory, with an element of surprise in the middle. There is also a hint of a stammer. One rendition could be: 'What should we do-oo?'

Woodpigeon

Since the Woodpigeon is always listed among the top ten commonest birds in Britain, it is very likely that you have heard this species in the garden. It is a useful sound to get to know.

The song has five notes – quick-slow-slow-quick-quick – and this sequence may be repeated several times in a row, with only a short gap between each delivery. The phrase has various renderings around the country, of which the best known is probably 'take-TWO-COOS- taffy', which gets the rhythm right, if not the words.

The song is delivered with a fulsome throatiness that is quite suggestive to some ears. It is certainly quite soothing and tuneful, and definitely less boring than the Collared Dove's refrain. The Woodpigeon makes one other sound, a wing-flapping to accompany its display (see pages 73 and 76). It gives the impression that the bird is geeing itself up, in the manner of a human sportsman or athlete clapping.

ABOVE LEFT: *The crooning sounds of Feral Pigeons are familiar to city dwellers.*
BELOW: *The Woodpigeon's throaty coo can be heard in almost any garden.*

Tawny Owl

The sounds of the night are confusing, and the position has not been helped by some erroneous information that has slipped into our culture and public awareness. Rule One: the Tawny Owl, the only owl found in most gardens, does not go 'tu-whit, t'-woo', as is so widely stated. It does go 'tu-whit' and it also goes 'woo', but it does not give the two together in sequence.

The 'tu-whit' is better rendered 'kee-wick!', with explosive emphasis on the wick. This is the Tawny Owl's call, used by members of a pair to keep in contact. The 'woo' is the fabulous, wild-sounding hoot you hear on the soundtrack of every horror movie (even those made in America, where the Tawny Owl does not occur). It is not actually given as a single hoot, but as a sequence of hoots, by the male. It is a gloriously atmospheric sound, too, with just the right tone for the mysterious night, uttered with a quavering shiver in mid-phrase.

The Tawny Owl has a wide vocabulary and you will hear variations on the above themes. Do not expect to hear any other species of owl in your garden because you won't unless you are deep in the country. The Screech Owl, often mentioned by country folk, does not officially exist under that name in Britain, but could refer to the Tawny Owl, or to the Barn Owl, a farmland bird that screeches with the best of them.

ABOVE: *Most owl noises in the garden come from the Tawny.* **BELOW LEFT:** *Young owls in and out of the nest make a whole range of insistent calls.* **OPPOSITE:** *Drumming not drilling – the famous drumming sound a Woodpecker makes is equivalent to a song.*

If you have Tawny Owls breeding nearby, listen out for the young uttering their begging calls on spring and summer nights. The sound is hard to describe, but the tone resembles the noise made by some children's squeaky toys when you squeeze them. Alternatively, if you make the slurping sound with your lips that anticipates a good meal, that is not far off the mark, either.

Should you hear the hooting of a Tawny Owl during the day, be careful that it is not actually a good human imitation. In fact, this applies to the night, too. A few years ago the newspapers reported on the story of two neighbours who, for many years, would customarily respond in imitative kind to a Tawny Owl that hooted loud and clear in their back garden. It was only some-time afterwards that they discovered that there was no owl in their gardens at all and never had been. The men had simply been calling to each other all the time.

Swift

You are most unlikely to hear this bird without seeing it. It makes a shrill screaming sound, unlike anything else in the garden. Once you have connected the call to the bird, it will become one of the sounds of summer.

Green Woodpecker

For some utterly inexplicable reason, the call of the Green Woodpecker is often known as a 'yaffle' and in former times the word was sometimes used as a name for the bird itself. But if you say, 'Yaffle, yaffle, yaffle' out loud, you will not get very close to what the Green Woodpecker actually sounds like.

The Green Woodpecker's advertising call is best thought of as a laugh. It is a ringing sound, going slightly up and then slightly down the scale. If you have heard it once, that should be enough to fix it the memory banks. In alarm the call is similar, but, perhaps not surprisingly, it has a more panicky, yelping quality.

Great Spotted Woodpecker

Woodpeckers are most famous for a sound that they make for only a very short part of the year, from January at the earliest to May at the latest. This is the celebrated drumming, which, in a Great Spotted Woodpecker, can be compared to a sudden burst from a pneumatic drill, the tone varying according to the type of wood the bird is striking. Sometimes the birds strike drainpipes instead, and in the past they have been known to strike milk-bottles! The overall drum-roll consists of about 12 beats altogether, delivered within half a second.

Contrary to what most people think, this is not the noise made by a bird making a hole. It is an intentional advertising sound. The bird is using a suitably resonant part of the tree as a musical instrument, just as some rainforest peoples traditionally beat tree-trunks as a method of communication. Remember, a drummer in an orchestra would get into serious trouble if he or she attempted to make a hole in their instrument!

Both sexes drum, and each individual's drum is apparently different, although the chances of detecting the differences by ear are very slight. Incidentally, when a woodpecker is making a hole, it does so with a series of sharp blows delivered slowly and irregularly, as if the bird were using a pickaxe.

Great Spotted Woodpeckers have a call note, too, which they usually utter when alarmed. And what other call could a wood-boring bird make than 'chip', as in woodchips?

Swallow

Learning the sounds of a Swallow is made easier by the fact that you can almost always see the bird. The song is quite a pleasing phrase and has a real galloping rhythm. The most interesting thing to pick out is that the song is different according to whether the bird is perched or flying. When perched, the bird keeps putting in little buzzes mid-phrase, as if it was having periodic attacks of flatulence (the Siskin, incidentally, does much the same).

Listen out for the sharp 'witt-witt' uttered by Swallows in flight. If you hear this call, look up. There might be a bird of prey about.

House Martin

House Martins do not sit around on perches singing in the same way that Swallows do – all of their meaningful sweet nothings are uttered within the nest, out of our audible range. In flight, they call to each other with short, somewhat dry, buzzy notes, sounding a bit like 'drrip, drrip' spoken quickly. At times you can hear this as a disembodied call from a migrating bird that is out of sight high up in the sky.

ABOVE: *The commonest call of the Swallow is a cheery 'wit-wit!'.* **BELOW LEFT:** *Male Swallows often sing from wires.* **BELOW RIGHT:** *House Martins make many intimate sounds from within the nest.*

Pied Wagtail

I used to live in West London where we had a little joke about Pied Wagtails. It so happens that the flight call of the Pied Wagtail is 'chizzick', which sounds the same as Chiswick, a place in the outer suburbs. You usually hear the call as the bird is passing over. It is, therefore, the Chiswick Flyover, a local monstrosity. Get it?

It's facetious, but it works – you'll remember it.

Pied Wagtails also sing, a little soliloquy of call notes run together in one huge sentence lasting 30 seconds or more, a sort of ecstatic babbling. But do not worry about having to learn it because you should be able to see the singer perched on your roof.

ABOVE RIGHT: *The loud song of the Wren is usually heard from low down in the undergrowth.*
BELOW: *The 'chizzick' call of the Pied Wagtail is easy to learn.*

Wren

If you hear a loud and very fast disembodied trilling phrase from low down in the bushes, it is very likely to be the song of a Wren. All the books comment that the song is unexpectedly loud coming from such a small bird, and that is absolutely right. It is just as well that the Carrion Crow's calls are not amplified in proportion!

A book cannot pin down a Wren song by offering a clear and unmistakable rendition, but it can offer some tips. For one thing, the Wren repeats the same phrase each time, like a political party offering a slogan. It has the same pattern: beginning, middle and end. It is shrill, fast and contains about 100 separate notes – no wonder that it can sound at times like an overexcited sports commentator describing the last few metres of a race. If you see the bird singing, it is clearly throwing everything into it, bill open wide, wings sometimes fluttering, body trembling.

One useful feature of most Wren songs is a very obvious trill somewhere in the middle part of the song – the 'twiddle in the middle'.

Only male Wrens sing, and they do it all year round. Both sexes also have a call that sounds like 'teck'. A few years ago, a Wren raised a brood in my garden and took up residence with its off-spring in my hedge. All day long, with only the slightest provocation, it would go on and on: 'teck-teck-teck…'

Dunnock

This is not an easy bird to recognize by voice because its songs and calls are rather similar to those of a good many other species. However, here are a few tips.

The song of the Dunnock is an inoffensive, reasonably tuneful, ditty lasting about five seconds. Each phrase that the bird sings is not dissimilar to the last, so you could say that its singing method is to repeat a slogan, rather like a Wren. The phrase is of similar pitch to a Robin's song, and it could be described as a quiet warble. What elevates it into a recognizable voice, though, is the Dunnock song's definite resemblance to the sound made as you push along a

trolley with squeaky wheels. Distinctively, the Dunnock sits on its perch to sing about five or six phrases, then moves to another song post and does the same thing, and so on.

The Dunnock's tricky call is a shrill piping, slightly broken in tone, sounding somewhat like an unoiled gate. It is a very common garden sound, especially in autumn.

Robin

The Robin's song is one of the garden's most important bird sounds to learn. No song in the garden is uttered for such a substantial part of the year. Only in late June and July, when the performers are moulting, is it missing from the garden's soundtrack. In August, September and October almost nothing else is singing except for intermittent outbursts from a Wren, so the calm, laid-back phrases you hear in the autumn are bound to be from Robins.

The song itself has a shrill tone, and it tends to give the impression of being a little melancholy, with a sighing air. When listening to a Robin, I always carry an image in my mind of a hippy-like bird lying back and smoking cannabis. Others find it more upbeat – perhaps it depends on your mood.

Leaving aside the whimsical, the Robin's song has a definite structure, characterized by long pauses between phrases, as if to leave time for

a response. The phrases themselves are so variable that, after every gap, the next one is quite different – longer, shorter, different – there is none of the slogan repetition of the Dunnock and Wren. A Robin song is like a series of questions in an interview, but without answers (unless another bird is responding).

Robins are highly unusual in that, come the autumn, all birds, both males and females, sing to defend a territory; in other species, males do all the singing, and only in spring. The song of female Robins is not recognizably different. The autumn bout of singing is said to be more melancholy than the spring chorus – but that view is highly subjective.

If you are listening to a Robin between December and March, look out for a subtle change in the perch used. When Robins are singing to defend a territory, they often sit down low, partly hidden by vegetation. But when a male Robin is singing to attract a mate he suddenly becomes an exhibitionist, performing from much higher and more conspicuous perches.

The Robin's call is simple, well-enunciated 'tick', endlessly repeated.

The Winter Nightingale

Bill Oddie once remarked that a common bird-related question he gets asked is: 'There is a bird that sings outside my house at night. Is it a Nightingale?' The answer is always the same: 'No, it's a Robin'.

Nightingales and Robins are close relatives, but Nightingales are rare woodland birds, not garden birds. Nightingales are also summer visitors that ration their song to April, May and June. Both species have large eyes for foraging in the low light of the woodland floor, and this talent enables them to be active at night. So it is the Robin you hear by the glow of your street-light or neon sign, whiling away the long hours of winter darkness.

OPPOSITE TOP: *The Robin's commonest call is a clear 'tick'.*
OPPOSITE BOTTOM: *When seeking a mate, a male Robin sings from a higher perch than usual.*
RIGHT: *If you hear a bird singing in the garden at night, it's a Robin, not a Nightingale.*

Blackbird

The Blackbird delivers by far the best and most accomplished of the garden's songs. Robins try hard, but they are not in the same class. If you can hear a rich, melodious, perfectly paced song, without too much repetition, it's a Blackbird.

If you are familiar with musical terms, the Blackbird is a contralto. It phrases are full of fluty whistles and fulsome warbles. The phrases are generally 1–3 seconds long, and, despite early promise, tend to peter out into a wheeze or a chuckle. In common with the Robin, a pause of a few seconds is left after each phrase, and the next phrase will be different from the last. Overall, Blackbirds sing with poise, control and the confidence of a virtuoso.

Blackbirds are major components of the dawn chorus, and they also sing again in the evening, when they can dominate the atmosphere. They have similar large, light-gathering eyes to Robins, allowing them to be active in the twilight.

If you have a very good ear for songs, you might find yourself able to distinguish individual

singers, since each bird has its own personal repertoire within the species' framework, incorporating its own recognizable catchphrases. Older birds also sound richer and more varied than first-years.

Blackbirds have several calls. For example, when alarmed, they storm into cover uttering a theatrical, panicky and very fast series of clucking, squalling calls. And they also have a bedtime roosting call, often heard in the evening in gardens: it is rendered 'chink, chink' and is quite an angry call, used by roosting birds to work out who gets the best perch for the night.

Song Thrush

The Song Thrush has a complex song – scientists tell us that each individual uses somewhere between 138–219 different song types – but it is fortunately a very easy vocalization to recognize. That's because of its unique rhythm and loud, urgent tone.

You can talk 'Song Thrush-ese' to yourself. It's simple, it's simple, it's simple. All you do, all you do, all you do, all you do. Is repeat. Is repeat. The short phrases. Short phrases. Short phrases. Short phrases. Several times. Several times. Several times. Several times.

That's all there is to it. The Song Thrush issues its phrases 2–4 times each, at a slow, steady pace, as if it were practising for an elocution lesson. No other garden bird has a song quite like it. The Song Thrush is a major player in the dawn chorus; indeed, many paired birds sing only at this time of day. To sing, a bird selects an elevated perch, often in full view of the neighbourhood, although it seems to sing less often from roofs than the Blackbird.

The call is 'tut' – almost exactly the same sound as you make when you are mildly irritated by someone or something.

OPPOSITE TOP: *Blackbirds often sing from rooftops.*
OPPOSITE BOTTOM: *A Song Thrush in full cry dominates the neighbourhood.* BELOW: *The Mistle Thrush is well-known for its habit of singing during inclement weather.*

Mistle Thrush

The efforts of this fine songster suffer when compared to the smooth accomplishment of the Blackbird and the distinctiveness of the Song Thrush, and from confusion with both. In the absence of these vocal rivals, we would no doubt cherish its song more.

The Mistle Thrush's song has a very similar tone to the Blackbird, but it is more repetitive, with favourite phrases coming up again and again. That is not to say that it falls into the stereotyped rote of the Song Thrush, it doesn't – the repetitions are not sequential. So you can see the problem. The Mistle Thrush is somewhere in between.

Here are a few tips. The Mistle Thrush's song has a definite melancholy air lacking in the more reassuring Blackbird, and it also has the odd quality of always sounding far off, even when the bird is close by. It is delivered more quickly than that of the Blackbird, with only short pauses in between phrases, and it is less clearly enunciated, more mumbling, than a Song Thrush's song. Importantly, the Mistle Thrush has a pronounced habit of singing when the others aren't or cannot. It can often be heard during the comparative listlessness of the afternoon, and the singers often perform nobly in the teeth of fierce winds and rain. In rural Britain this has earned it the nickname 'Storm Cock'.

The species' call is distinctive, and all too familiar if you have Mistle Thrushes nesting in the garden. It is a loud, dry rattle, similar to those old football rattles that are now out of fashion. It is an angry sound, often delivered loudly but fitfully as if the bird was spluttering with rage.

An October Night

Apart from owls, Robins, Nightjars and Woodcocks, few birds seem to stir in the dark, but do not forget the sounds of the avian 'motorway'. Go out on a calm, brittle October night, with the stars out and frost in the air. Leave the comfort of your home between nightfall and midnight, walk into the garden, and prepare to hear a sound from a wild, barely-known place. If you listen carefully for about 10 minutes, you will probably hear the 'seep' of a Redwing. If you are lucky, it may be accompanied by the 'schack' of a Fieldfare, or even the 'tsee' of a Blackbird. The Redwing's call, though, will be the most prevalent sound. You may hear it every few minutes, or more.

The birds uttering these calls are travellers: night migrants. Redwings flood our country in October and stay for the winter, fleeing the frost and intense cold of their native Scandinavia. Once here they are nomadic, flying from place to place in search of berries. They travel on a broad sweep, and there is not a household in Britain over which these birds have not flown many times.

Up above your garden, then, is an invisible motorway some 500 metres (1,640 feet) above you, carrying intensive bird traffic. The flow is greatest in the early part of the night, but there will be some movement throughout. No person has ever travelled along this stream, where the winds and the perspective are different and there are no signs to direct you. It is a wild place just above your own familiar patch of ground. Go back inside, stilled, and wonder.

Fieldfare

You will not hear this winter thrush call very often from your garden, but it makes a pleasing, frothy 'shack' or 'schack-schack-schack' in flight, the notes running rapidly together.

Redwing

The Redwing has a sharp, high-pitched call that could be rendered as 'seep!' It has a vague similarity to the sharp intake of breath you make when you touch something hot or prick your finger.

Blackcap

When they visit gardens in winter, Blackcaps are not exactly boisterous, and you might miss out on hearing their call. For the record, it is a sharp 'tack'.

In fact, this sound is really convenient for the birdwatcher. If you take the last vowel in the names of the Blackcap, Wren and Robin respectively and use it to amend the consonants tck, you will end up with the relevant call: BlackcAp – tAck; WrEn – tEck; RobIn – tIck.

Spotted Flycatcher

The most common call from this flycatcher is a quiet 'wiss-chook', with the emphasis on the 'chook'. It also makes a whine similar to an exhalation of breath through a blocked nose – the sound of someone breathing when they have a cold.

The male does have a song, but it is absolutely terrible, at least to our ears. Delivered at a slow pace, it is just a few short, squeaky notes run together to make a series: 'schlip; schlurp; schlip; schaa; schi.' It sounds vaguely like the cheeping of a sparrow, but is higher-pitched and heavily distorted. At the end of each series is a hesitant pause, and no wonder!

Long-tailed Tit

If you look up the call of the Long-tailed Tit in most bird books, you will find yourself being misled. They almost always describe the call as a trisyllabic 'see-see-see', muttered quickly. Well, I have heard an awful lot of Long-tailed Tits in my time, and unless my ears have a very specific fault, Long-tailed Tits typically run four notes together, not three – they go 'see-see-see-see' repeatedly. This is the dominant sound made by individuals in flocks to keep in contact. Say it aloud and you'll master the Long-tailed Tit's main call.

The species also has two others. One appears to be used in the context of concern or anxiety, and that is a short, spluttering sound – 'trr'. If, when you say this out loud, you spit out some saliva, you have the right idea. The other call, used by relaxed birds in conversational mode, is a gentle 'tupp'.

OPPOSITE: *Listening in the garden at night can be a real adventure. You might also catch sight of an owl!* ABOVE: *The Blue Tit makes a bewildering number of sounds.* BELOW LEFT: *Separating the different calls of birds in a flock can be a daunting challenge (here 2 Blue Tits, Coal Tit and Goldcrest).*

Blue Tit

Identifying the sounds of tits is a huge problem, and the Blue Tit contributes more headaches than most. The sages assure you that Great Tits are more confusing to listen to as they make a vast number of different sounds. So they do, but at least their main spring song is readily recognizable, unlike the nearly unfathomable Blue Tit.

The songs of the Blue Tit tend to have a trilling format and in the most prevalent song heard in spring, three extended notes precede a long trill on one note – 'deee-deee-deee-diddle-diddle-diddle'. It is fast-paced and has a light, airy quality.

In alarm, the Blue Tit has a memorably long, scolding call, which it utters when it becomes afraid or annoyed.

Great Tit

The Great Tit makes one of the most dominant sounds of spring, and it is essential that you learn to recognize it early on. The two-note chime is heard in just about every garden from January to June, and sometimes again in autumn. It can be accurately rendered as 'TEE-cher, TEE-cher, TEE-cher…' and it has also been likened to the sound of saw-sharpening, or a rather cheery siren.

Certainly the song's structure, two notes of different pitch alternated a few times, is similar to that of an ambulance siren, but it is usually only a few seconds long. Beware, too, that birds regularly change the pace and tempo of their singing. However, the song is always distinctly happy-sounding and there is something of an attack on the first note ('TEE'); both of these features distinguish it from the very similar song of the Coal Tit.

Another useful mnemonic for the Great Tit's song is that is sounds like a foot-pump being used to put air into a tyre. A Great Tit in my own garden can vouch for the similarity, having definitely responded to the sound of me filling a tyre by bursting into song!

Great Tits sing from high perches and may carry on all day long. Each male has 2–6 different song types, so expect to hear a few subtle variations on the general theme described above. In addition, Great Tits are rumoured to have 40 calls and can even hiss like a snake, so perhaps it would be wise not to worry too much about learning them.

Coal Tit

Identifying this species' song will always be tricky because it is so similar to the Great Tit's efforts, both in structure and tone. One useful clue is that, should the two-note chime be uttered from the top of a coniferous, not deciduous, tree, it will probably be a Coal Tit.

Other than that, the Coal Tit's song is softer and squeakier than that of the Great Tit. It sounds more like a bicycle pump than a foot-pump, too, if that's any help.

The calls of the Coal Tit include a distinctive 'twEE?'.

ABOVE: *The Great Tit's song is strident and cheerful.*
LEFT: *The Coal Tit sounds more squeaky.*

Nuthatch

The Nuthatch is a noisy bird with a wide vocabulary. The most common call is a cheerful 'toowit, toowit!' (say it quickly) that is very like a human whistle. If you half-say and half-whistle the word, it will come out in about the right way. This is the most important call to learn.

In spring, Nuthatches sing a numer of songs, the commonest of which is a whistled trill, similar to a tuneful pneumatic drill. They also sing a slowed down, slurred 'pee-ew, pee-ew, pee-ew', similar to one of the elements often heard from a Song Thrush.

One clue that might point towards Nuthatch is a loud, cheerful voice hidden by treetop leaves. When singing or calling, the Nuthatch does not usually show itself.

Jay

If you ever wondered how the Jay got its name, try saying its name out loud in the angriest voice you

can muster. The name is onomatopoeic, although you could be forgiven for not realizing it.

The Jay's thoroughly rasping sound is easy to recognize and is wholly discordant. And, like a defective car alarm, the over-cautious Jay can be set off by the very slightest disturbance.

Magpie

In contrast to the Jay, you can usually see a Magpie at the same time as hearing it. Its call is a mischievous, machine-gun-like, rattling 'cha-cha-cha...' that will be familiar to most garden bird enthusiasts. The Magpie also makes little clucks, often heard as it flirts its tail.

ABOVE: *The Nuthatch is noisy but often difficult to see in the canopy.*
LEFT: *Magpies chatter in a mischievous way.*

121

Carrion Crows often begin the day with their own harsh additions to the dawn chorus. Unfortunately, this passes their apparent irritation onto people rudely woken from their slumbers.

Jackdaw

The Jackdaw more or less goes 'Jack!' to call out its name. At least, it calls out half of its name, for in truth the sound is a bit more like 'kya!' It is both abrupt and somewhat upbeat.

Learning this species' call really shouldn't demand too much concerted effort, especially since you will normally see the birds doing it. Who said that bird sounds were difficult?

ABOVE LEFT: *The caw of the Carrion Crow is rendered all the more emphatic by the way it thrusts its body forward while calling.* **BELOW:** *The Jackdaw's name is onomatopoeic: it says it.*

Rook

The Rook is a member of the crow family, and, as one might expect, it makes a sound very similar to a caw. At times you won't be able to tell the difference from the familiar sound of a Carrion Crow. However, the Rook's caws have lost their edge when compared to Carrion Crow calls. They are softer, without the angry tones. The Rook has evidently gone to the counsellor to seek help, and all the irritation has slipped away from its voice.

At rookeries the din is remarkable, and a good many uncrowlike noises echo through the tree-tops. In particular, the birds often include some high-pitched dissonant calls of the sort that come from choirboys whose voices are in the process of breaking.

Carrion Crow

Carrion Crows caw, and that's pretty much it. If they are on their territory, they will often belt out their caws in threes, each one emphatic and irritable. If you see them doing it you'll notice that they lean down and forward, thrusting out each note.

ABOVE: *When a Starling flaps its wings while singing that is a sign that it is yet unpaired.* **BELOW RIGHT:** *'Cheep!'*

Starling

The Starling is justly famous for its ability to imitate the noises in its environment. Over the years Starlings have been known to mimic the clucking of chickens, the crying of babies, the hoot of owls, the ring of trim-phones (remember those?) and, most recently, the sound of car alarms. It is rumoured that a Starling once caused a football match to be halted because it kept imitating the referee's whistle.

Engaging and fascinating though this ability is, it is a bit of a red herring when it comes to learning the actual song of a Starling. The imitative element is only a small part of this bird's output, and even without it, the Starling is one of our most unusual and entertaining singers. Where else could you hear a bomb drop and a whistle go off amid a stream of lively babbling and chattering?

The Starling often sings from rooftop aerials, and it doesn't take a huge leap of imagination to picture it tuning into the airwaves and spewing out a mixture of white noise, wow and flutter. Not surprisingly, this is usually a very easy bird to recognize.

Starlings often sing in chorus, especially when they gather for a communal wash and brush-up prior to going to roost. In spring, however, from late January onwards, males perform alone on branches and rooftops, close to a potential nest-site. You can tell whether these singers are paired or not. If they are bachelors, they often accompany their vocal output with a display of flapping wings.

House Sparrow

Not even those of us who love our sparrows could possibly hold these birds up as great vocalists. Great talkers, yes – their cacophonous chattering from the security of a dense bush can be deafening – but, considering that they are technically songbirds, they are a bit short of musical merit. In fact, there is no doubt that they coined the word 'cheep', and that's about the extent of their talents.

When a House Sparrow calls to another it goes cheep, and when a male is advertising for a mate it sits by a nest-site and goes 'cheep-cheep-cheep!' This song, incidentally, is usually delivered on autumn mornings.

Chaffinch

Hopefully, you are a cricket fan, because in order to appreciate what is probably the best description of the Chaffinch's song requires a little basic knowledge of our summer game. The accelerating rattle and final flourish of the Chaffinch's phrase has been likened to the accelerating footsteps of a slow bowler approaching the crease, and then delivering the ball.

Chaffinches are unusual among the garden's regular singers in that they only begin to perform in earnest in February, although there will be the occasional practice sessions beforehand. At its best, the song is a dominating, cheerful phrase, repeated over and over again, although most males have several favourite (and usually pretty similar) phrases.

Young Chaffinches have been shown to learn their songs from their father and his neighbours, so song types are passed down generations and often develop into local dialects. In theory, it should be possible to distinguish a London Chaffinch from a Sheffield Chaffinch. But for now, identifying the Chaffinch as a Chaffinch should be enough. The Chaffinch has lots of calls, but the best known is a very happy-sounding 'pink-pink'. Coincidentally, this is also the colour of the male's breast.

ABOVE: *The Greenfinch has a 'chip-chip' call note.*
BELOW LEFT: *The Chaffinch is an enthusiastic spring singer.*

Greenfinch

Suburbia suits Greenfinches, and their trilling songs and calls are very much part of the garden soundscape. The last sentence perhaps underlines part of the problem in identifying these birds – their calls tend to blend in.

If you have ever kept a Canary, you will have a head-start in learning the Greenfinch's sounds, because the two species are closely related and their voices quite similar. The Greenfinch is less adventurous vocally than the Canary, confining its song to a series of rather dry-sounding trills on different pitches and at different speeds.

Interspersed within these trills, however, is a quite different sound: a long, drawn-out wheeze – 'greeeeen!' It has been likened mischievously to the sound of a constipated human being attempting to push, and it is a particularly regular addendum to the normal song in spring.

Greenfinches often sing in flight, and they are not, like many suburban residents, too proud to sit atop a Leylandii cypress. In fact, have a look at any bird sitting on this plant, and it will probably be a Greenfinch.

Goldfinch

The Goldfinch is one of those enviable characters that not only looks stunning but sounds delectable, too. Its song is based on its twittering call note, 'tickelit', and is simply lots of these calls liquidized into a pleasing, flowing ramble. The tone is quite similar to that of a Wren, but is more modest and less in-your-face. The song is euphonious but only moderately distinctive, so you will need to get a look at the singer the first few times you hear it.

Bullfinch

This is a quiet bird and you may well receive many visits before you ever hear one calling. It simply gives a soft but far-carrying 'pew' call, with a slightly mournful ring.

ABOVE: *Goldfinches are usually silent when they are feeding.* BELOW LEFT: *Groups of Goldfinches often indulge in a bit of community singing.* BELOW: *Bullfinch.*

Birds through the Seasons

One of the delights of birdwatching is that things keeps changing, month by month and day by day. Nowhere is this more apparent than in the garden, where we as householders can witness important events in the lives of our birds and follow their progress first hand. After a few seasons of careful watching we can get a feel for what is happening at certain times of year, and can appreciate how the breeding season, for example, or the winter season is unfolding. In the following pages, to help this progress along, we give you an idea of what to look out for in the garden month by month. It will apply most precisely in suburban Central England, so if your garden is in the north of Scotland you can make allowances for your later spring.

ABOVE : *Bullfinch.*
OPPOSITE: *Lengthy periods of snow spell trouble for our garden birds.*

January

You might think that for a garden bird there was not much difference between December and January, but you'd be wrong. The winter solstice on 21 December marks the real New Year for birds, the point at which day-length at last begins to increase again. This triggers much physiological activity, and ultimately amounts to the birds getting into breeding condition. One of the most important tasks is for the birds' sexual organs – which shrivelled almost to nothing in the post-breeding period – to regrow and be brought into working order. This process goes under the fantastic technical name of photoperiodic gonadal recrudescence.

For now, though, visible bird activity will be in thrall to the weather. Good days, with sunshine and blue sky, will trigger plenty of song, and even some courtship display among the fitter, more experienced members of the community. Blue Tits may visit nest-boxes, and Magpies and Carrion Crows may bring sticks to their nests to begin spring refurbishment. In rural areas, Rooks are attending their colonies and doing much the same thing. Very few birds breed, except for the occasional pair of frighteningly productive pigeons or doves.

On more typical January days, when it is cold and grey, birds are on something of a treadmill. The smaller ones must eat from dawn to dusk more or less without stopping, and they must get up earlier and roost later than they would in summer, relative to sunrise and sunset. All this is to ensure that they have enough to eat to keep their 'inner fires' burning through the long nights. However, pigeons, plus finches such as Siskins and Redpolls, can store a little excess food intact in their crop or gullet, to be digested at times throughout the night, and larger birds, such as Carrion Crows or Blackbirds, usually have more than enough reserves to last them into the following day.

Not surprisingly, the bird feeders will be busy, especially in the morning, afternoon and also, curiously, at around midday. This unexpected middle peak may arise because birds at the bottom of the garden's hierarchy, or pecking order, take their turn, giving them a rare, unmolested visit to the feeders. Some species of bird also follow a daily path, like a milk round, visiting your garden at a certain time before moving inevitably on, so this may lead to different peaks of activity. On the other hand, Robins, Wrens and Blackbirds will stay put, and, where necessary, they will evict visitors of the same species.

Sounds to listen out for

The start of the singing season for many birds, including Blue, Great and Coal Tits, Starling, Nuthatch and Dunnock. Great Spotted Woodpeckers begin drumming. On fine days pigeons and doves will coo.

LEFT: *Many garden birds, including the Great Tit, start singing in January.* **OPPOSITE:** *Bullfinches often visit early spring blossom and buds – much to the chagrin of some gardeners, as these birds can be destructive.*

February

Spring is unveiled in layers and February reveals further cracks in the erosion of the winter, the process that began in January. Bird display intensifies further when the weather dictates that it can, and more and more species and individuals take part. This is the first month that you can see Blue and Great Tits perform their short, whirring song flights; Dunnocks may wave a wing at each other (see page 83). These latter birds are about to enter into a very complicated breeding season.

For most of the winter many birds in the countryside have been relying on the fruits of the previous autumn – the last few berries, nuts and seeds. Now, though, these supplies are dwindling fast, and many birds begin to move about more, seeking out places that they had not previously checked in an effort to find some fantastic Shangri-la overflowing with supplies. This, inevitably, brings more and more birds into gardens, where reliable food indeed fulfils their dreams. Some of these newcomers are very noticeable – Siskins, for example, and Fieldfares and Redwings – but others, such as nomadic Blue Tits, Blackbirds or Reed Buntings, are less so. Whatever the origin of the visitors, February can be one of the most exciting months for the garden enthusiast.

If there is a single salvation for the berry-eaters, it is that much-maligned and overlooked creeper: ivy. Strikingly different to most berry-producing plants in sending forth its fruits from January until the spring, ivy attracts many customers at this time of year, including Blackbirds, Robins, Blackcaps and Woodpigeons.

Ivy aside, the garden does make a moderate effort to provide other attractions for birds. Snowdrops and crocuses bring along the odd dozy fly, as does the blossom on the fruit trees, forsythia and magnolia, but it's not much yet. One of the birds that does benefit, though, is the Bullfinch, which settles on a variety of trees to munch the buds and flowerheads.

Sounds to listen out for

The birdsong chorus is swollen by Chaffinches and Blackbirds, two species that start up in earnest this month.

March

Apart from those species that winter overseas and are yet to arrive, every garden bird is now embarked upon its breeding cycle. Some birds are forming pair bonds, some are nest-building and a few lay eggs before the end of the month. All this activity makes the garden a busy place.

Birds such as sparrows, various pigeons, Jackdaws and Carrion Crows stay together as pairs throughout the year, and remain within territories recognized and generally respected by others of their species. For these birds spring is a gentle affair, blissfully free from mate seeking. They concentrate on courtship manoeuvres that strengthen the pair bond, and, importantly, carry these out to ensure that both sexes are physiologically compatible with one another – the chemistry, you see, can follow the action. So Tree Sparrows and Collared Doves sit side by side, as if their arms were round the shoulders of their beloved; Jackdaws mutually preen; and Carrion Crows whisper croaky sweet nothings to one another in the privacy of their treetop nests, already finished.

For other birds, pair bonding is not yet complete. Dunnocks, in particular, enter into various different domestic arrangements. The females defend large territories in the late winter, and now, in March, it becomes a male's task to move in with

ABOVE: *A rookery is full of activity in March. The first eggs will be laid mid-month.* **BELOW LEFT:** *A Long-tailed Tit with one of the 2,000 or so feathers that it will use to line its nest.* **OPPOSITE:** *A Blue Tit in spring finery.*

the incumbent female and take over the defence of the boundaries. What happens next depends on the quality of the male. Some take over the whole territory successfully, while others find it too large for them to defend, and recruit one or even two male helpers to lend a hand; inevitably, these share the female's affections. In addition, a few males manage to take over the territories of two females, and in doing so, monopolize their affections. All of this drama is worked out with much wing-waving, making the Dunnock one of the most intriguing garden birds to watch at this time of the year.

Species that are well beyond this preliminary stage include Tawny Owls, Kestrels, Long-tailed Tits, Mistle Thrushes and Rooks. These birds, for various reasons, complete their nests in March and may lay eggs. The Long-tailed Tit starts early because its complicated nest takes three weeks to build and must be ready on time. Mistle Thrushes and Rooks build early to make sure there are plenty of earthworms available in the soil for the young, while the ground is still moist.

Tawny Owls and Kestrels start early because these predatory birds find it easier to catch food for the young before the spring vegetation has grown too thick and impenetrable.

Sometimes birds start early for no reason other than being ready as individuals and pairs. Among them may be Robins, Blackbirds and Song Thrushes, but never tits, which time their breeding to coincide with the glut of caterpillars later on in May and June. The birds that start early are usually experienced, older individuals that have made it through a winter before and wish to have a bumper breeding season. A March start may mean that they eventually bring up three broods in a year.

Remarkably, this breeding activity occurs during one of the leanest feeding months of the whole year. We may associate the dark days of December or January with food shortages and a natural cull of birds, and so we should, but March is almost as bad. The natural food supplies have almost died out and they are being replaced only slowly by an increasing population of insects. Both this month and next are full of hardship. So don't put the bird feeders away just yet, they are an important source of food and will keep some birds alive that would otherwise have succumbed. Other birds, faring better, will be able to get into breeding condition earlier than they would have without your generosity.

Finally, the very first summer visitors usually turn up in March. The occasional Swallow makes an appearance in a garden somewhere before the month is out and Chiffchaffs may sing their metronomic songs from the flowers of willow trees – a focus of activity, incidentally, for many birds at this time.

Sounds to listen out for

If you are lucky, you might hear an early migrant Chiffchaff repeating its name; in most gardens you won't hear it again until next spring. If you have Mistle Thrushes in your area, you are likely to hear them calling a great deal this month, as they have begun nesting.

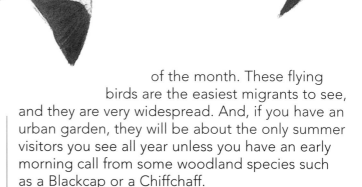

April

Many a birdwatcher wishes that every month was like April – the pastime becomes as easy as selling ice-creams on a hot day. Birds can be seen everywhere. They are in fresh spring finery, they are very noisy, and they are not yet fully concealed by freshly grown leaves. To make themselves conspicuous they are displaying, bickering, nest-building and coming back and forth to feed young. It's all just too easy.

And one of the month's greatest delights is the return of well-loved species from their winter retreats in Africa or southern Europe. Having spent many months in warmer climates, these summer migrants are indicators of the passage of spring, and their presence in your garden can make the advance of the season all seem wondrously personal. There is something about a visit by a Swallow, whisking over your rooftops on its way north, that makes the spring 'official' – you have not planted or tended a Swallow like you have your garden plants; it is authentically wild.

Look for Swallows from the first week of April. House Martins, their close relatives, will arrive a week or two later; Swifts follow at the very end of the month. These flying birds are the easiest migrants to see, and they are very widespread. And, if you have an urban garden, they will be about the only summer visitors you see all year unless you have an early morning call from some woodland species such as a Blackcap or a Chiffchaff.

If you have a more rural garden you can effectively clap the birds in as they arrive, one by one. Blackcaps and Willow Warblers roll in during the first week of April, Whitethroats in the second, and towards the end of the month you can also see Cuckoos, Turtle Doves and Spotted Flycatchers. It is an annual miracle to see so many species suddenly populating vast areas of the country, and your garden is part of that extraordinary phenomenon.

Another key feature of April is the amount of birdsong. If you are not normally particularly sensitive to natural sounds, April is the time to give bird songs a try, since the vocalists really are shouting at you – they can on occasion interrupt conversations across neighbourly garden fences. Don't expect to identify all of the species, just enjoy them for their aesthetic appeal. Bird songs can be heard everywhere at the moment, and even in the most urban of gardens there will be an unmistakable broadcast of natural music, playing all day long.

April is a key breeding month, with the majority of species laying eggs at some time during its 30 days. For example, Blue and Great Tits, which raise only one brood a year, begin laying their eggs somewhere around 5–10 April. Other species that will be producing eggs include Chaffinches, Wrens, Robins, Blackbirds, Starlings and Magpies.

Female Blue Tits take a week or so to complete the clutch and will then begin incubation. During this time the male will often bring food in to the sitting female – so do not be fooled into thinking that the pair already has young, it is too early. Greenfinches, Goldfinches and Robins do much the same thing.

Although April is usually rather a dry month in general, it is famous for its showers; indeed, April weather, especially the temperature, will have a crucial effect on the breeding success of our garden birds and affect their whole seasonal productivity. What they want least is any extended period of cold weather in April, with wind and rain. It makes food harder to find, partly because insects are less active in the cold and partly because wind and rain make foraging more difficult. And although many birds' eggs will not have hatched, the sitting bird may be forced by hunger to abandon the clutch for a short time, just to keep itself alive.

Sounds to listen out for

Redwings may gather together and chatter in chorus, as if discussing their forthcoming journey back to Scandinavia or Iceland.

OPPOSITE TOP: *The Swallow is one of the most popular heralds of spring.* **OPPOSITE BOTTOM:** *A Song Thrush incubates its eggs.* **BELOW:** *A Blackcap may contribute to the dawn chorus in larger gardens.*

DAWN CHORUS

Every garden should be able to witness some kind of dawn chorus, although inner-city areas and those lacking trees will be restricted to just one or two species performing. Nevertheless, it is well worth making the effort to listen to the early morning outpourings of birds, wherever you are.

At any time in the spring you will need to get up before it gets light, and in May that can often mean about 4.30am. But make yourself do it, at least once a season. It will be worth it, really. Besides, you won't have far to go to make yourself a cup of reviving coffee, and eat a hearty, well-earned breakfast with the sense of triumph that you've had the willpower to do it.

Don't ever try to learn songs during the dawn chorus. Lots of people attend special dawn events, fully expecting to start recognising the various species. However, you are no more likely to become an expert in identifying birds on a dawn chorus outing than you would become fluent in any foreign language in one session of an evening class. In fact, it will be worse. At dawn a whole load of individuals of every species are all singing at once, and it's totally confusing.

But that's also its charm. The dawn chorus is an experience, not a tutorial. Enjoy the first notes uttered in the pitch darkness, then the gradual swelling of sound, until it can become almost deafening. You'll also see your garden and your neighbourhood in a different light, when all is yet to stir.

May

May is the sort of month where, everywhere you look in the garden, something is happening. You might notice a Wren creeping through the ivy, its bill full of food for its youngsters (it will probably be a female, since male Wrens are slouches when it comes to feeding offspring). You might notice a female Chaffinch among the fresh spring leaves of a tree, helping itself to some caterpillars during a break in incubation. You might see a male Blackbird bringing an earthworm to a newly fledged youngster while, at the same time, his mate is already sitting on their next clutch of eggs. And you might look up to the sky and see your first Swift of the year flying over the rooftops, recently arrived from its long journey that began a month or two ago in Africa. This fair-weather bird is one of our last migrants to arrive.

Despite the fact that most birds are dealing with eggs or nestlings in May, male birdsong reaches its spring zenith. That's because territories still need to be protected, and any slip in security now could spell disaster for a lazy male, with itself and its mate ousted at a critical stage in the

breeding season. Continuing to sing may bring other benefits, too. Birds such as Blue Tits, Starlings and Swallows are forever on the lookout for liaisons with willing females, of which there are usually plenty. Of all the eggs laid in an average garden in an average spring, a high percentage are not genetically those of the male to whom the female is socially paired.

A good many of these eggs hatch in May, or at least they are supposed to, but a garden spring is full of small disasters. Eggs may be infertile in the first place, or the parent may incubate them poorly, regardless of the weather. And, of course, there are nest predators about. Gardens, unfortunately, with their rather limited cover, make good places to look for occupied nests, however well hidden they may appear to be. So May is the month when the Magpie gains its bad reputation as a bird killer, together with the Jay, and both species will take eggs and live young. Grey Squirrels may be serious nest predators, and, in rural gardens, so may Weasels. Occasionally, the Great Spotted Woodpecker may hammer through wood into the nesting chamber of tits, and take the young to dismember and feed to its own offspring. Hazards are everywhere.

Miraculously, though, eggs do hatch into nestlings without being seized by a bill or claws, and that spells hard work for parents. Tits are famous for making up to 1,000 visits a day to feed their young, but most species are less feverish, dispensing more food at a time and making fewer trips; they usually have fewer young to look after than tits, as well. It's all a question of strategy. Tits have but one brood a year, to coincide with a glut of food, and they can raise a dozen or more young at a time (although 7–8 is more frequent in gardens). But Blackbirds, Robins and pigeons may have 3–4 broods a year, producing almost as many young, but distributed over several attempts. Those in the latter category spread their costs, gambling less than tits.

Sounds to listen out for

Birdsong drenches the garden, since just about every species is singing. The dawn chorus is cacophonous, but, for once, singing continues just about all day. Blackbirds, Song Thrushes, Robins and Great Tits will probably be the dominant vocalists.

June

June is a month when numerous young birds leave the nest to become fledglings. They spill out somewhat, facing the world in a poorly feathered, half-ready state, with short wings and short tails. Their first enemy is starvation, since most young birds leave with few fat reserves; but soon, should they survive the ordeal of their first day and night out of the nest, an army of predators will be after them. Sparrowhawks are one example. These hunters time their late breeding season especially to coincide with the peak emergence of young, inexperienced birds that are easy to catch.

Partly through bulk production and partly though an innate urge to survive, fledglings do make it through their first few days, and soon the June garden will take on the look of a nursery, with parents and young everywhere. Most small birds feed their fledglings for at least a week after leaving the nest, and usually rather more. Young tits, which fill the air with their frothy begging calls, have abundant caterpillars to look for in the trees, so they become independent within a few days; you can recognize them by their yellow cheeks. Blackbirds and Robins, with more sparing amounts of suitable food available, take rather longer. In a few of these species, the male takes the lead in feeding the brood so that the female can get into breeding condition for another nesting attempt; gradually, as they go down their parents' list of priorities, the fledglings of even these species get the message and leave.

One species in which the young leave remarkably soon is the Starling. These brown versions of the adults receive very little post-fledging care. Instead, they gather into flocks of their peers after just a couple of days, and travel well away from the garden in search of grassland or fields.

OPPOSITE: *A Blue Tit on one of its many feeding visits to the nestlings – up to 500 a day per parent!*
ABOVE: *Not quite adult, a Starling with a mixture of milky brown juvenile plumage and the adults' spots.*

Fledglings can cause a problem for garden birdwatchers. They invariably look a bit different in plumage from the adults, and it is very easy to mistake them for another species, or be completely flummoxed. Juvenile Robins, for example, lack the red breast of maturity, and instead are covered with pale spots. Young Blackbirds are also speckled, making them look more like Song Thrushes. Young Wrens don't look right, while Dunnocks are heavily streaked, Greenfinches aren't green and Mistle Thrushes look very strange indeed.

Sounds to listen out for

Listen out for two common sounds: the purring 'churr' of young Starlings begging for food and the calls of young tits up in the trees doing the same thing.

July

For some birds July marks the end of their breeding season, and they can metaphorically sigh with relief. Tits, Carrion Crows, Great Spotted Woodpeckers and Magpies have done their stuff, and will hope to try again next year.

For many others, though, there is still another brood to raise, or perhaps even their first. Swifts start late and the development of their young is very weather-dependent: their offspring may have to remain in the nest for nearly two months after hatching. Spotted Flycatchers, too, having arrived from Africa later even than Swifts, will normally have their first set of young leaving in the early days of July, and many pairs audaciously attempt another brood shortly afterwards, despite the time constraints. These birds, plus multiple-brooded Blackbirds, Song Thrushes, Swallows, Dunnocks and pigeons, will remain preoccupied by the mad frenzy of production throughout July. There might even be some redemption for a few birds that failed to find a mate the first time round, which find themselves unexpectedly in demand at this late stage due to death or divorce from previous partners.

Some species would actually consider July to be their peak breeding season. These include Woodpigeons, whose clapping display flights and soothing songs are a feature of this time of year, as well as Greenfinches and Goldfinches. All are dependent on grain or seeds, and with harvest time approaching, Woodpigeons will soon find it exceptionally easy to find enough food for them to create milk for the young. As for Goldfinches, they are awaiting the annual crop of thistles. Both species, of course, will circumvent the need to find wild food if there is plenty available in the garden.

By the month's end, the garden and its surrounds will be brimming with birds both young and old. They will not all be familiar faces because the late summer triggers a widespread phenomenon known grandly as post-juvenile dispersal. This is a great movement of recently fledged juveniles away from their parents' territory. Newly independent, the youngsters go on the equivalent of a gap year, travelling no more than a few kilometres

from their hatching place, but putting distance between themselves and their families nonetheless. Dispersal gives young birds the chance to explore potential future territories for themselves to claim in the spring, and it also ensures that the chances of inbreeding are greatly reduced.

Many of these youngsters roam around in flocks. It is very useful for them to do this because they can learn different foraging techniques and feeding sites by watching each other at work. So an exciting feature of a garden in July or August will be the flocks of juvenile birds passing through, all excitedly feeding as they move around the neighbourhood. There may be as many as 100 individuals in such gatherings, and quite a few species. Tits usually form the core, and birds such as Treecreepers, Goldcrests, Willow Warblers and even Lesser Spotted Woodpeckers may be carried along with them. Who said July birding was dull?

Sounds to listen out for

Sleepy July resonates to the reassuring, unhurried song of the Woodpigeon. Many a garden will witness the 'see-see-see-see' calls of Long-tailed Tits travelling in parties through the neighbourhood, often in company with other tit species.

August

In August the garden can seem deserted; it's certainly at its quietest in terms of songs and calls. The bird feeders may see their worst business of the year, and generally the garden experiences less obvious activity than usual.

This has less to do with real numbers than with behaviour. August is the time of the annual moult, when every garden bird is exchanging old feathers for new, kitting itself out in a wardrobe to take it through to next spring. Much as we might delight in this makeover, to birds it is an exhausting time, when considerable energies are diverted into growth, leaving little for anything else. It is comparable to human adolescence and the birds, like their teenage counterparts, feel listless and irritable. Many will stay under the shade and cover of tired, late summer vegetation, and not show themselves much. For a few weeks they lose their exuberance and are also very vulnerable to the usual garden predators. It's best for them to keep a low profile.

One event that does draw birds out from the bushes is the swarming of ants. On special days in the summer, flying ants emerge from their underground colonies, filling the skies in an effort to find a mate. It is like the arrival of an ice-cream van on a street full of kids. Swifts and House Martins have a field day, gulls wheel overhead, and a good many less-than-expert aerial fly-catchers try their hand at snapping the insects in mid-air. House Sparrows, for example, try to emulate their more aerodynamic garden neighbours by sallying upwards on over-flapped wings and too short tails, like middle-aged men suddenly taking on the parallel bars.

August is often hot and dry, and if such conditions persist, it can cause garden birds problems. Song Thrushes, for example, cannot find enough worms on dried-out lawns, and they are forced to call upon their fall-back strategy, which is to seek out snails. Even Blackbirds, though highly resourceful, may be affected. Others, though, revel in the conditions, especially Swallows and House Martins, for whom the gentle summer breezes under clear skies make feeding easy.

The bird bath or pond may be the centre of any activity there is. August is a good month to watch birds drinking and bathing in the bird bath, sometimes almost at the same time. House Sparrows will often bathe in patches of dust instead, and several bird species may indulge in sunbathing – ruffling their feathers, spreading their wings and tail, and lapping it up. Birds don't have many idle moments (unless they are House Sparrows), but these days of late summer allow for a few.

Sounds to listen out for

At the end of the month you might begin to hear young Great Tits delivering a few teacher phrases, in readiness for territorial battles in the months ahead.

OPPOSITE: *A rare sight in midsummer: a Blackbird allows ants to crawl all over it and squirt acid on its plumage. 'Anting' probably helps to remove unwanted parasites from the bird's plumage.* **ABOVE :** *A Goldfinch feeds its young.* **LEFT:** *Birds sunbathe too! This is a young Blackbird.*

September

This dynamic month, part-summer and part-autumn, heralds great change in the garden. Some birds settle in, to be part of the scene for months to come; some pass through; and some depart.

The process of migration has, in truth, been going on since late July, but it becomes ever more obvious now. Swallows and House Martins, in particular, may stream over the rooftops on their journey south, the initial part of which is quite leisurely. And if you look up, you might realize that, almost overnight, the Swifts have gone. Never entirely trusting of our climate, they have stolen away and are an unusual sight in September.

If you are a birdwatcher, rather than a gardener who watches birds, you will be more aware than most of September's potential for heart-thumping encounters with migrants. Even a garden in the most mundane setting may offer unexpected appointments with birds that are normally found far away. Lesser Whitethroats, Reed Warblers, Pied Flycatchers and Redstarts are among the species that sometimes call in during August or September. In the light of such possibilities, you can become a

ABOVE RIGHT: *A familiar sight in September: Swallows gathering on wires prior to their migration.* **BELOW:** *In autumn food is everywhere.* **OPPOSITE:** *Winter thrushes migrate over on still autumn nights.*

real birdwatcher in your garden, doing things you might normally do on the coast or by a reservoir: you rise at dawn, you keep your binoculars or telescope within easy reach, you check the weather, and you look skywards. If you do all these things you will find something good, that's for sure.

The great dispersal of this year's juveniles may still continue right through September, but the birds concerned will no longer look like juveniles. They have lost the badges of childhood – no more spotty Robins or brown Starlings – and are now difficult to tell from adults. The sharp-eyed observer may notice the dark bill and brownish wings of a young male Blackbird, for instance, but most of the year's freshers at least have the uniform, if not the experience, of adulthood. Some of them, at least, will quit their wandering lifestyle and settle into the garden, intending to stay thereabouts. The more confident ones, some individual Great Tits, for example, will even sing a few phrases to lay a territorial flag down for the next breeding season. It's a cocky message of ownership that, for the moment, goes unanswered by hard-nosed adults.

September sees the wrapping up of the breeding season. Goldfinches, Bullfinches, House Martins and Swallows may all have young in the nest at the beginning of the month, but these broods will be their last and, at least in the case of the aerial species, the offspring face an uncertain future.

Sounds to listen out for

Nothing much is singing, except Robins.

October

Many an October day begins with the deceptively gentle song of the Robin filling the damp air. These birds are unusual among our garden residents in that they are aggressively territorial in the autumn and winter as well as the spring, defending a special feeding territory. Their casual autumn ramblings are a smokescreen for feelings of intense possession and threat, like diplomatic statements from countries on the brink of war. They sing to keep potential rivals at bay, but if the vocal statements don't work, fights readily break out in the shrubbery.

It is the height of the fruit season and almost everyone is cashing in. If you have berry-bearing shrubs in the garden, you cannot miss the Blackbirds, Song Thrushes, Starlings and pigeons gorging themselves, and the undercover raiders, whose plunder of the fruits is a little less conspicuous, include Robins and Blackcaps. Berries are an excellent source of nutrition, and for birds their presence in such abundance makes it a lot easier to get into top condition for facing the tough months ahead.

Berry-laden trees and shrubs, in common with any concentrated food source, may form the stage for skirmishes between birds attempting to cash in on the bonanza. Both Blackbirds and Fieldfares will occasionally hold a short-term territory on a particularly choice hedge or tree, but their efforts tend to be frustrated by the sheer numbers of potential shoppers. Not so the Mistle Thrush; this is a large and aggressive bird, and it can more than hold its own at a berry source. Indeed, in October these heavily built thrushes adopt their own trees and requisition them for exclusive use, both in these days of plenty, and, more importantly, well into the winter.

It is not only berries that cause headlines in October. Other nuts and fruits are also plentiful, and many woodland and garden birds have strong associations with them. The Jay, for example, collects acorns for its winter store, and the Nuthatch collects beech and hazel. In woodland, the strength of the beech crop is an important factor in the winter survival of a wide range of species, including our familiar Great and Coal Tits.

Indeed, you might have cause this month to ask where many garden birds are. Although the autumn is not as quiet as the middle of summer, most garden enthusiasts notice a paucity of visitors to the artificial feeders. The answer, of course, is that birds have less need of your generosity when the countryside is overrun with produce: you cannot sell sand at a beach. The tits and finches are elsewhere, on an autumn gastronomic cruise through the area, but before long they will be back, with begging bowl freshly polished.

Remarkably, given that the breeding season is well over, several species of bird pair up in the autumn, especially youngsters. House and Tree Sparrows, for example, spend sunny mornings singing next to a breeding site before going off to spend the rest of the day feeding. Rooks serenade in the treetops, bowing and trying to beguile. Mallards on ponds flirt and posture. Birds, it seems, never quite leave thoughts of reproduction behind, whatever the season.

Sounds to listen out for

Owls begin to hoot in earnest.

November

Most people think that, by now, migration is done and dusted, and that all the migrants have gone 'home' to Africa. This could not be further from the truth. There is plenty of bird movement going on in October and November, but the cast of characters is different from the usual Swallows and Cuckoos, and the birds' destination is different, too.

Far from having our bird pool drained by the onset of winter, we stand on the edge of the chilly European continent as a major receiver of visitors. Millions of birds, edged out by periods of frost and cold, cross the English Channel to spend the winter in our mild, damp climate. It may not be perfect here, but there are lots of berries, short-lived frosts and rarely much more than a few flurries of snow, at least in the southern half of our island. Swallows may head for South Africa, but Black-headed Gulls, Blackbirds, Chaffinches, Goldcrests, Mallards, Song Thrushes, Redwings, Fieldfares, Siskins and Skylarks are perfectly content with Middle England. From October and November onwards, our gardens are potentially full of these immigrant European birds.

The garden residents have largely settled in. Our bird tables and hanging feeders are beginning to become a bit more popular, partly because the birds need them more, and perhaps also because their value needs to be proven to the new arrivals in the garden, especially the youngsters. By the time November arrives they are hooked; there will

ABOVE : *In November the feeders become active again after an autumn lull. This visitor is a Nuthatch.* **BELOW LEFT:** *Gulls often fly over gardens on winter days.*

be few days when they do not visit that great rarity in a bird's life, a reliable food source.

As the days shorten, the rhythms in the garden become more constricted, and patterns may emerge more clearly than in previous months. Bird feeders will have busy times and less busy times; the birds will rise earlier; song, such as it is, will peak at dawn and dusk; the last hours of daylight are full of activity and birds visibly collect at roosts.

November is a good time to watch commuters. In many parts of inland Britain, gulls fly over in large V-shaped flocks on their way to a lake or reservoir for the night; Starlings head into town; Pied Wagtails may make their way to a greenhouse or flat roof; and Jackdaws and Rooks weave circles in the air as they prepare to bicker over the best tree perches in their communal roost. These last species are still making noise after dark, like young kids on the first night of an adventure holiday.

Sounds to listen out for

Not much is singing, apart from the Robins and Wrens. But on fine days, especially early in the morning, Song and Mistle Thrushes begin their singing season, albeit haltingly and briefly at first.

December

December has a reputation for being a month that is hard to appreciate. It's too blank and too dull. One month too many before the New Year, December is best over and done with.

We don't know if the birds feel like this, but we can guess that they do. December contains the shortest days of the year, when the light is at a premium and birds are at roost for longer than they are able to feed. A bird's daily life is in thrall to the night, and how to survive it. Bird feeding stations may be active all day, as birds try to gather the reserves to fuel them through the interminable night. They may feed feverishly, but their natural exuberance is dampened.

Sometimes, though, this last month of the year livens up. Harsh weather is not desirable for the welfare of our birds, but it can make garden birdwatching much more interesting. For one thing, visitors come to the garden in much greater numbers and variety than usual; the weather may push in special visitors such as Reed

ABOVE : *A Robin feeds in the December gloom.*
BELOW LEFT: *Mild days in December may see Magpies indulging in some nest refurbishment.*

Buntings, Pheasants or even Waxwings. Garden watchers may even be able to observe 'escape movements' in which large numbers of birds, mostly ground-feeders, fly by day to escape unexpected sharp frosts or deep snow, and may stream over in vast numbers. These can be exciting times.

Almost unnoticed, Robins in the garden may begin to act strangely. The males suddenly shift to singing from higher perches and they become tolerant of company, sitting side by side with a stranger on a spade. Some Robins, even in these difficult times, are pairing up – an early sign of spring!

Sounds to listen out for

December nights are long and quiet, but a Robin might offer a few hesitant phrases, encouraged by the lights at a window or on the street. Heard in the dead of night, these sweet sounds are often accredited to Nightingales, but that songster is long gone from these shores, feeding on beetles in Africa, and is not set to return to Britain until April. The garden often sounds dead at this time, although the Carrion Crow's caws and the Jackdaw's sharp exclamations may break the silence. In the countryside, Rookeries are full of throaty, noisy exchange.

Chapter 5

Providing for Birds

This chapter looks more closely at what you can do to encourage the birds in your garden. Since there are innumerable books written on this subject, we're going to adopt an approach that is a bit different; namely, we will focus on why certain foods or nest-sites are appropriate for the birds concerned. What is it about a tit's lifestyle, for example, that makes it such a common visitor to hanging feeders? And what is it about nest-boxes that makes them appropriate for birds? We will take a bird's view of garden provision rather than reel off the usual list of appropriate foods.

ABOVE: *It's easy to provide food for a Woodpecker...*
OPPOSITE: *...But you won't attract Kingfishers unless you're close to a river.*

At this point, it may be useful to remind ourselves of our garden birds' basic needs:

- Food to eat, which can be provided directly through bird tables and hanging feeders, or indirectly by cultivating plants to encourage insects or provide fruit
- Water to drink
- A place to build a nest and raise young
- A place to roost at night or loaf during the day
- Facilities for feather care, such as a bird bath or earth for dust-bathing
- As far as possible, safety from garden predators, especially cats

Obviously, you will not be able to provide all of these things for every bird species. Gardens are not, for example, appropriate places for Black-headed Gulls or Green Woodpeckers to nest, although these species might use our backyards for feeding; equally, you cannot easily provide a roosting site for Swifts since they often sleep up in the air. So the following accounts are specific and brief. In order to avoid repetition, they are also divided into groups, rather than by individual species.

It is, of course, also quite possible that you may want to discourage certain species from visiting because of the damage they may do in the garden. If this is so, I refer you to the next chapter.

Finally, a word about expectations. Regrettably, as far as your garden is concerned, you are completely at the mercy of your immediate environment in terms of what birds you see. City gardens and rural gardens naturally have different visitors, and it will be very discouraging if you try to attract birds that have little chance of visiting your garden. For example, you might be desperate to attract a Treecreeper, so you paste suet in tree bark day after day and buy an expensive specialized nest-box that you fix lovingly on an appropriate tree. But your efforts will work only if there are Treecreepers in your area.

The golden rule for obtaining the maximum enjoyment from the birds in your garden is: have low expectations, but await surprises.

Water Birds

It may be stating the obvious, but you cannot seriously attempt to attract many water birds without being adjacent to suitable habitat such as a river or lake. So Mallards, Moorhens, Kingfishers and so on are off the agenda for most gardens.

However, if you construct a large pond from scratch, you could conceivably tempt in the odd Grey Heron to take fish and frogs within a year or two, and a Pied or Grey Wagtail will very likely take to wandering around the margins. If that happens, you deserve congratulations.

If there already are water birds in your neighbourhood, all you have to do is throw out bread or grain regularly to enjoy Mallards, Coots and Moorhens feeding on your lawn.

LEFT: *The Moorhen is a regular visitor to lawns and borders, so long as these are near water.*
OPPOSITE: *A bird-friendly garden pond.*

A Garden Pond

Creating a pond is arguably the most bird-friendly change you can make to any garden. Best of all, it can be done in a couple of days. A pond, uniquely, adds a completely new habitat to the garden, and the birds cannot fail to benefit. The water will attract a wide range of invertebrates that would otherwise be absent, and the permanent source of fresh water will be used by many birds for drinking and bathing. For the latter, it is important that the pond has a 'shallow end' with gently sloping sides. If you forget this bit, you will be disappointed with the birds' response. The details of pond-digging are beyond the scope of this book.

Suffice it to say that you cannot just dig a hole and fill it with water (well, you can, but it won't last long). It is best to use butyl rubber as the lining, which is available from garden centres, although it is not cheap. Any vegetation you put into the pond should preferably be native – but don't plunder it from the wild. Be careful not to locate the pond in shade, since the mini-ecosystem needs sunlight to prosper, and try to keep it away from trees. If you don't, you will spend many hours clearing away the autumn leaves, and regret that you ever had the idea. Finally, fun though ponds are, they are potential dangers for young children; if you have toddlers around, do not even contemplate constructing one.

Birds of Prey

The only bird of prey that you are likely to attract into your garden from scratch is the Sparrowhawk, and that's easy enough to do. You simply put up bird tables or hanging feeders and it will soon find them and start helping itself to the smaller birds.

Sparrowhawks rely on regular gatherings of birds within their home range and they make a habit of flying into flocks rather than attacking individual birds. Occasionally, Kestrels copy Sparrowhawks' ambush style of hunting, but they are not very efficient at catching birds. They prefer small mammals, caught from above.

Some gardeners will be more interested in preventing these birds of prey from taking too many of 'their' small birds. There is a discussion of this topic in the next chapter (see page 164–7).

If you have a large property with some big trees, or if you have access to the roof of a large building, you could try helping Kestrels by putting up a nest-box. Kestrels are common and adaptable birds, but they do suffer from a lack of available nest-sites, so you could benefit this bird greatly if you do so. A suitable box is of the open-fronted type (for more details, consult a suitable title in the *Further Reading* section – page 172). Sparrowhawks, incidentally, almost invariably nest in woods.

Pigeons and Doves

The sad truth is that most people don't really want to attract pigeons to the garden (see page 165). These birds do have an unfortunate tendency to take over a bit, and they can easily monopolize the bird feeders for long periods of time.

However, some people take pigeons to their hearts, and in this case the tastes of both are easily satisfied. Pigeons are ridiculously easy to attract to feeders because, in contrast to most other garden birds, they are specialized in the consumption of a single, widely available food item: grain. Cheap

seed mixtures containing wheat or other materials are ideal and so, indeed, is bread.

Pigeons will use any level surface for feeding, be it the ground or a bird table, and some will even call at hanging feeders, with much flapping and limited success. They are not very good at using these, as they a bit big for the average feeder. Having said that, Woodpigeons often feed on berries in trees, sometimes hanging upside-down like a tit or a small finch.

In common with other seed-eaters, pigeons appreciate water where it is provided. These birds have a habit of visiting water to drink, only to be seduced into having a bath by the irresistible sight of the lapping wavelets. The bath may well need a refill after a pigeon or dove's visit.

If you wish to encourage breeding by pigeons, the three species have slightly different require-ments. The Feral Pigeon uses buildings, especially window-ledges, although you could also provide a dove-cote. The Woodpigeon nests on the branches of medium-sized to large trees. The Collared Dove, although using much the same sites as a Woodpigeon, very often chooses a small coniferous tree as the base for its nest, especially early in the season.

ABOVE : *A large open-fronted nest box on top of a pole may attract a pair of Kestrels.* **LEFT:** *It's not hard to attract Feral Pigeons to the garden!*

Tawny Owl

Tawny Owls are highly sedentary birds that settle into a territory early in life and may live there for up to 10 or even 20 years, often outlasting the human residents of a neighbourhood. They have a catholic diet of small mammals, birds, frogs, fish, worms, insects – and practically everything else that moves – and they are adaptable enough to cope with most circumstances. They will hunt at your bird feeders, for example, especially at dawn. Their only requirements are plenty of bare ground, leaf litter or short turf over which they can hunt, and tall, densely leaved trees in which to roost and nest.

If you don't have owls you cannot do much to attract them, and in any case they can take a long time to move into an area, whatever you might provide for them. However, they will take to chimney-type nest-boxes, and will use them both for breeding and for roosting in winter.

RIGHT: *Few feeding challenges defeat the Great Spotted Woodpecker.* **BELOW:** *Room service: a Tawny Owl brings food to the nest.*

Woodpeckers

Recent studies have shown that woodpeckers are exceptionally intelligent. You wouldn't think that clinging on to trees and banging your head against them was a particularly cerebral activity, but the woodpecker has to learn about the food sources in its territory, what they are, where they are and how to deal with them, and that needs brain power.

Up in the trees, Great Spotted Woodpeckers employ a lot of skilled feeding techniques. They will often lodge seeds in a fissure to get purchase for opening them, for example, and they are highly capable of hanging from twigs and branches to lap up insects from the surface of leaves. Their very strong feet and the unusual arrangement of their toes (two face forwards, two back) give them exceptional clinging power, although they have difficulty in perching across a branch in the way that most birds with 'normal' toes do.

All this should serve to explain how easily the Great Spotted Woodpecker takes to bird tables and hanging feeders. It inhabits a territory that it knows so well that, should you provide new feeding opportunities, it will be aware of them almost immediately (so you can try squashing suet into bark, for example). Normally the only thing that will hold a Great Spotted Woodpecker back is its reticence; it is also foiled by some anti-squirrel feeders with protective grills.

Perhaps surprisingly, given its ability to excavate holes for breeding and roosting, the Great Spotted Woodpecker will sometimes use nest-boxes, providing these are fixed to high branches. They must also be filled with polystyrene chips, though, so that the birds can fulfil their urge to excavate first!

The Green Woodpecker is different in character to the Great Spotted, since it acquires most of its food from lawns and pasture. Make your lawn as free from herbicides as you can, and drop the occasional apple near a favourite ant-guzzling spot.

Aerial Birds

It is surprising to think how comfortable our aerial birds – Swifts, Swallows and House Martins – are with people. They all preferentially use artificial places for their nests. Yet their main foods, aerial invertebrates, are not found in any special density around human dwellings, except perhaps farms with livestock. In fact, if anything, urban and suburban habitats suppress the insect fauna.

Nonetheless, House Martins use the eaves of houses for building their mud nests, Swallows use rafters and Swifts use crevices in towers. You can obtain specialist nests or nest-boxes for House Martins and Swifts; the former are especially useful for keeping the messy visitors tidy. All three species are regularly colonial, so, for House Martins in particular, it is no good put-ting up just one or two boxes on your walls. Buy a cluster.

RIGHT: *Swifts need high ledges for breeding. They often nest on church towers.* **OPPOSITE TOP:** *It's hard to tempt Wrens away from the security of thick bushes.* **OPPOSITE BOTTOM:** *A well-resourced Dunnock is a well-behaved Dunnock!*

Swallows tend to nest under cover in various outbuildings, including sheds and garages. This is fine, but if they do so they will need permanent access throughout the breeding season. If this means leaving doors and windows open you might have to think about the security implications.

Ponds or even puddles are very attractive for aerial birds, the former as feeding, drinking and bathing sites. In April, House Martins and Swallows will require mud for their nests – so make sure that you hose down a section of earth if the weather has been unusually dry.

Pied Wagtail

Pied Wagtails are terrestrial birds designed for a life of walking. They can perch, but usually shun branches; hanging feeders are incomprehensible to them. Bird tables are usually off their radar, too. But they like the simple things in life, such as a few minute crumbs scattered on the ground, or the insects accumulated by the side of a pond or stream. They adore roofs, presumably because these are easy to check for insects, attract the heat of the sun, and are not the natural habitat of human beings.

'Pied Wags' also use the garden for nesting. Ivy on walls is ideal, but they occasionally use plant pots and other strange places.

Wren

If you are to understand the world of a Wren, you have to use your imagination. This is one of our smallest birds, so to a Wren a bush is a capacious building and a garden is as big as a park.

Metaphorically speaking, this species lives its life among 'buildings', moving back and forth among the corridors of tangled vegetation and feeding on the lower ground floor among the leaf litter. It seeks out invertebrates, mainly, picking aphids and caterpillars off leaves and snatching small beetles and spiders from their hiding places in the half-lit world of the bush and scrub interior. Much of the business of a Wren's life – the feeding, singing, preening, roosting and building of nests – takes place just a few centimetres off the ground. To a Wren, the top of a tree would be as tall as the highest building. It just doesn't go there: it is an alien world.

Once we understand the secretive nature of the Wren, we can guess that it would be reticent about using bird feeders, high up in the air and out in the open: such a place would be anathema to the agoraphobic. A Wren does occasionally snap up the smallest crumbs spilt by the feeding birds above, but usually only if it can remain close to cover. It will rarely, if ever, join the hordes above because, although it can punch well above its weight, that is usually not enough.

Most gardens have Wrens that thrive without help, but if you are fond of them you can grate some cheese and throw it into the leaf litter under a bush; an alternative is oatmeal. Apparently, turning over the compost heap will reveal plenty of goodies that they can find easily. More indirectly, you can provide that which is most important to this species: dense undergrowth such as hedges, creepers (especially ivy) and herbaceous borders.

Dunnock

The Dunnock to some extent shares the Wren's world of undergrowth and leaf litter, although it is not quite so afraid of showing itself and will sing out in the open at the top of a bush. Most people's experience of the species is of a bird feeding on

the ground, furtive yet confident, clearly visible beneath the bird table.

This species has a very thin bill and can deal with only the smallest items. Peanuts (except fragments) are beyond its scope, but it has taken well to nyger seed and sunflower hearts, comparable in size to the tiny weed seeds that it typically takes in the wild in winter. In summer, its diet consists of very small insects, and here a delicious possibility arises – in theory you can affect the life of a Dunnock more than you might imagine.

As mentioned on page 83, Dunnocks have a variable mating system in which birds of either sex may find themselves in relationship with one, two or even three mates. It is thought that this system originally derived from the difficulty Dunnocks have in providing sufficient food for the young, given that the parent birds can pick up only small items in their bills. This problem pushed females in the direction of mating with more than one male to ensure that the male workforce helping in food provision doubled, or even trebled. The more males that were under the impression that the junior genetic material was theirs, the more the chicks would benefit.

In particularly rich habitats, though, this does not need to happen. Where insects truly abound, it is possible for a conventional pair of birds to find and transport enough food to supply their young. So if you have plenty of native bushy vegetation in the garden, copious leaf litter, and no pesticides or herbicides, you should be able to keep your Dunnocks honest!

Robin

This iconic garden bird is the dream of every backyard enthusiast because not only does it respond to our various attempts to please, it also apparently comes to say thank you – or so it seems. Its tameness is proverbial, at least in Britain (it is much more reticent in mainland Europe). More readily than any other garden species, it will come to the hand for mealworms and potter at our feet for crumbs.

At the risk of sounding like a bit of a killjoy, your Robin may not benefit by being tame and confiding if there are cats in your garden, as it will become much more vulnerable. In such situations, it might be best to attract it to the bird table instead, where it will come for bird cake, grated cheese, breadcrumbs, nuts and, especially, fat. A few Robins have been seen attempting to master hanging feeders, but this is highly unusual. The Robin is a perching, not a clinging, bird.

At night, Robins sometimes shelter in sheds or greenhouses, and this habit could conceivably help them through the winter. In the breeding season, the same outbuildings are regularly used for nest-sites, so make sure that the birds have access such as a window, without compromising your security arrangements. The Robin is not an especially adventurous or imaginative nester in the wild, usually hiding its structures amidst thick vegetation close to the ground, so it is odd that in gardens it has a reputation for occupying all sorts of unusual sites – coat pockets, open drawers, tins, shelves, and so on; presumably these locations must be safer than most. Whatever the reason, this inventiveness is just another attribute that has endeared the Robin to gardeners everywhere.

LEFT: *Gardens suit Robins perfectly, and it's easy to encourage them to breed.*

Thrushes

Thrushes live in such comfort in gardens that anything you do to help them will be the icing on their cake. Blackbirds, for example, breed more successfully in suburban gardens than anywhere else – even the wildest and richest forests far from human habitation. Both Blackbirds and Song Thrushes adore the patchwork of trees, bushes and lawns that abounds in suburbs of a certain age. The modern trends in estate housing, which lead to a more open-plan arrangement with smaller gardens, are not so favourable. But, so long as your garden has some grassy or earthy open ground, plus bushes or hedges in which the birds can nest, roost or feed undercover, you have a winning combination.

The Blackbird is one of the major users of a garden lawn. As such it will benefit from an organic approach to lawn care, with minimal use of herbicides or pesticides, or even better, none at all. It also benefits from regular mowing, of course. In addition, it feeds among leaf litter and it will benefit if the plants in your garden, especially the shrubs, are native. Blackbirds nest in dense shrubbery, such as hedges, and also roost there, as well as in evergreens. In autumn they feed from berry-bearing shrubs and in winter they take a very wide range of artificial foods, including bread, fat and scraps, taking them from bird tables or the ground. All in all, there is plenty you can do for Blackbirds.

The Song Thrush is ecologically similar to the Blackbird, but, to ensure that it can use its unique talent for breaking snail shells open, try to make your control of slugs as organic as possible (although so far there is no proven link that slug pellets harm thrushes). This species is a much less regular visitor to bird tables than the Blackbird, being shyer and more nervous, but it will come to ground stations for scraps. This could be important because it has a much more limited diet than the Blackbird. It also requires denser, shadier and more hidden nest-sites, places such as creepers or deep inside trees. In early season, it may well use a young conifer. Song Thrushes, like Blackbirds, use mud in their nests, so if you spot one beginning to build, make sure there is some on hand.

The Mistle Thrush is less of a garden bird than the other two species, and the main way it can be attracted is by growing berry-bearing bushes, especially hollies or yews.

ABOVE: *Thrushes are attracted to berries in autumn and winter.* **LEFT:** *All a Blackbird needs is a lawn free of chemicals and thick bushes nearby.*

In view of this bird's secretive habits, it is remarkable that, in the last 30 years, it has become a regular visitor to bird tables and hanging feeders, where it often feeds on peanuts, as well as raisins and 'softbill' mixes. Extraordinary.

Goldcrest

The smallest bird in your garden is specialized for life in conifer trees. With its small size and thin bill, it is adapted to picking among the needles of pines, yews and spruces for insects, as well as their larvae and eggs. At times, especially in winter, it will venture into broad-leaved trees and even bushes, but these cannot supply breeding sites. The birds nest in dense foliage well above ground.

The good news for garden enthusiasts who would like to see Goldcrests is that a single large conifer in the neighbourhood will be enough to sustain a breeding pair throughout the year, and from this base they will visit even the smallest conifer plantings, including Leylandii hedges.

In winter, Redwings and Fieldfares rarely feed on bird tables, but they will visit for berries in the autumn and then, later in the winter, come down for apples and other fruit thrown to the ground. Collect some of these in the autumn so that, in February or March, you will have a ready supply.

Regarding berries, it should be noted that some are more popular with thrushes than others. The birds usually come for red or blue ones, so don't plant white-berried shrubs such as snowberry if you want to attract birds. If you wish to please all the thrushes, you will need to provide berries of different sizes, and plenty of them. Good berry-bearing trees or shrubs include elder, hawthorn, holly, cotoneaster, honeysuckle and ivy.

Blackcap

The Blackcap earns its living skulking around bushes for insects or fruit, usually remaining inside the leaf canopy and rarely showing itself. It gleans insects from leaves anywhere from the canopy of a thick tree to the lower depths of the herbaceous border. It does not, however, feed on the ground. Blackcaps feed in autumn on small berries such as elder, and take ivy berries in spring.

And so, if there are suitable trees nearby, you are bound to attract them.

The Goldcrest's investigative and systematic way of feeding ensures that it will know all about your garden layout and feeding stations, too. It occasionally comes to crumbs on bird tables and has even been recorded at hanging feeders. Nothing that requires perching and clinging skills will be beyond this species, although the food – such as a 'softbill' mix, for example – needs to be appropriate.

Spotted Flycatcher

There's only one thing that really interests fly-catchers in your garden, and that's the supply of flying insects. True, these birds often nest in open-fronted nest-boxes, and, especially, various creepers along walls. But what brings them to gardens in the first place is enough food for themselves and their young.

To impress Spotted Flycatchers, plant native trees or shrubs, dispense with any insecticides, and add in a few showy, insect-attracting plants such as Buddleia or lavender.

Long-tailed Tit

Long-tailed Tits have astonished scientists recently by acquiring the habit of visiting peanut feeders. Had the birds been reading the books, as they should have been, this would never have happened! It clearly states in the relevant tomes that these birds remain insectivorous throughout the year. So the records of birds taking nut fragments, breadcrumbs and grated cheese have caused something of a stir.

One thing that certainly predisposes Long-tailed Tits to using hanging feeders is their acrobatic nature. The long tail is used as a counterbalance, enabling the birds to perform gymnastics in the treetops and reach everything they need among leaves and on twigs. It was always likely that, once a suitable food was found for them, these birds would cope with artificial dispensers easily enough, especially those hung from the trees like extensions of branches. Popular trees for insect-feeding include oaks, birches and willows.

You will not be able to attract Long-tailed Tits unless the habitat around you is suitable. The birds live in flocks, and each flock has its own wide territory encompassing a considerable number of deciduous trees and bushes. Your garden really needs to be part of that territory already if you are to see this species at all, let alone feed it.

If Long-tailed Tits are present and you have a particular dedication to them, you could consider providing them with a thick, low, thorny bush in which to conceal their nest (they don't use holes like other tits). Gorse or brambles are ideal if you can bear them, or you could try Pyracantha. The thorns are essential to keep out cats and Magpies, which are frequent predators. At the appropriate time, in March, it is also worth sprinkling some small but fluffy feathers on the ground to help the birds with their nest-lining.

OPPOSITE TOP: *Redwings feeding in the leaf-litter.* **OPPOSITE BOTTOM:** *A Goldcrest ventures away from its conifer home.* **ABOVE LEFT:** *The Long-tailed Tit is a surprisingly versatile garden bird. This one is about to take suet wedged in the timber.*

Other Tits

Tits are among the most abundant of all garden visitors, and usually the ones that find new feeding sources first. It is their curiosity that makes them pioneers. In woods and hedgerows they investigate every possible refuge for insects and nuts – leaves, trunks, branches, needles, herbs, leaf litter and the open ground – and this habit makes them come across feeders in the natural course of their wanderings.

Tits are also small birds and highly acrobatic. Their legs and feet are very strong, and some have ridges on the underside of their feet to help them cling. All hang upside-down effortlessly, and the smaller species can work their way along to the very ends of thin branches. No wonder that, no matter what challenges we may set them, tits will usually find and utilize our food sources.

Blue and Great Tits feed on very similar foodstuffs, including scraps, fat and suet as well as their more favoured nuts and seeds. Peanuts are always popular, and the Great Tit will often come to the ground for these; black sunflower seeds, with their high oil content, make particularly nutritious alternatives.

Both of these tits readily take to nest-boxes in preference to their natural tree holes. The two species compete with each other for them, and the Great Tit is always dominant. For this reason,

ABOVE: *The Blue Tit is often the first to a newly placed feeder...* **BELOW LEFT:** *...And is closely followed by other visitors such as the Great Tit.*

vary the size of the entrance holes: Great Tits need holes of at least 2.8 centimetres (1.1 inches) in diameter, whereas Blue Tits will take anything in the range 2.5–3.5 centimetres (1–1.4 inches). Do not provide too many boxes – one or two in the average garden is best – as these birds are territorial. Whatever you do, never put up one of those dreadful bird-table-and-nest-box monstrosities that you can buy from garden centres.

Coal Tits are smaller than the other species and are adapted to feeding among conifer needles, which makes it quite surprising that they are often such regular garden visitors. Although their main food is insects, they do take seeds and nuts in autumn and winter, and particularly favour black sunflower seeds on the feeder.

It can be difficult to get Coal Tits to breed in the garden because they are usually out-competed by the other species. However, if you have a conifer tree on your land, try fixing a nest-box on it, down low; that will be an open invitation to a Coal Tit in preference to the others. You can also try using a box with a smaller entrance, say 2.4 centimetres (0.9 inches). Always place it low because, in the hierarchical world of tits, the strongest get the penthouse suites and the weakest get the basement.

Nuthatch and Treecreeper

These two small birds spend much of their lives holding on close to tree-trunks and searching for insects on the surface and in fissures. Both rely on plenty of trees being present in the garden, and the Nuthatch needs large, mature broad-leaved ones such as oaks and beeches. One major difference between the two species is that the Treecreeper is largely insectivorous year-round, while the Nuthatch, true to its name, feeds on nuts in the autumn, winter and early spring.

If you have Nuthatches in your neighbourhood (if not, bad luck, because these birds are highly sedentary and do not colonize new areas quickly) it is not difficult to tempt them to your feeding stations. They manage hanging feeders effortlessly, as you'd expect, and are also able to feed from bird tables, a consequence of their need to search for nuts on the ground. Nuts, seeds and fat are all popular as foodstuffs.

The Nuthatch is extraordinarily fussy when nesting. Apart from having large deciduous trees available for nest-holes (it will take to nest-boxes), it also needs a conifer tree nearby to provide flakes of bark for the nest-lining and a ready supply of mud to mould the entrance hole to exactly the right size.

Treecreepers are much less 'natural' garden birds than Nuthatches and will not come to feeders, although they might conceivably investigate the pole supporting a bird table! If you have these birds nearby, allow them

ABOVE: *Most crows are not especially welcome in gardens, except perhaps for the mild-mannered Jackdaw.* **BELOW LEFT:** *The only way to 'feed' Treecreepers is to wedge suet or fat into the cracks of tree bark.*

to find artificial food in the course of their usual checks over the surface of bark by smearing on fat or wedging nuts in cracks. You can also erect special ready-made nest-pockets for them.

The Crow Family

You might not think that it is entirely appropriate to include crows among the list of birds to attract to the garden. They hardly need much encouragement to visit, feeding readily on lawns or at bird tables, usually in the early morning, and eating every kind of foodstuff. Carrion Crows use tall trees for their nests and Magpies use smaller ones, both of which are usually found in abundance in suburban areas.

But you might want Jackdaws to nest nearby. These gentle crows make their nests in holes, usually in trees but often in chimneys. They should be discouraged from doing the latter because their way of beginning to build a nest is to throw sticks down the chimney until one lodges and can be used as the start of a foundation! Try providing a suitable nest-box next to a chimney, or attach it to a large tree-trunk.

155

Starling

You might not entirely like the sight of a gang of Starlings gobbling up food that you have earmarked for more 'desirable' species, but the fact is that, at present at least, this species is in decline and needs our help. Nobody is entirely sure of all the causes of the Starling's ill-fortune, although some suggestions put forward have a lot to do with the garden environment.

For instance, Starlings are primarily ground-feeders that are drawn to rough pasture, and this includes lawns. The evidence suggests that the less management a lawn has had in the past the better it will be for Starlings in the present. Needless to say, promoting the invertebrate abundance and diversity that Starlings relish, means no more chemicals; it actually means less mowing, too, but that may be socially unacceptable.

Moreover, Starlings have begun to face a dearth of nest-sites. The problem is that our houses and estates are too tidy. Starlings like old-fashioned eaves and unsightly holes, the sort of things not featured in the house or garden makeover programmes. They like cavities in outbuildings and in dead or dying trees. If you cannot bear to look at such things, then why not provide nest-boxes?

ABOVE: *Starlings need crevices in eaves or trees for nesting.* **BELOW:** *A lawn free of pesticides will be a draw for Starlings.*

The birds are usually colonial, so provide several on one trunk of a tree, for example, or on the side of a building. They need to have an entrance hole of at least 5 centimetres (2 inches) in diameter and a depth of 30 centimetres (12 inches).

ABOVE: *A little untidiness about your buildings will help the House Sparrow.*

Sparrows

The House Sparrow is one of the few species that you can give bread to without any feelings of guilt, although in fact bread is not that bad, so long as it is soaked in water before being presented to the birds or, better still, ground down to crumbs. A good many city sparrows probably survive – and have done for many years – on little else. Sparrows also feed on a variety of other scraps, plus fat, suet, bird cake, seeds and peanuts. They are nothing special in terms of perching ability, but manage well on most bird tables and hanging feeders.

Recently, House Sparrows have been in decline and their plight has hit the headlines, but people are still not sure why the numbers are slipping. It seems unlikely that you can do much to change your garden to reverse the situation. However, if you have got sparrows you can help them by putting up nest-boxes for them to stuff with hay; you can provide hay as well, if you don't mind the mess. The birds are colonial, so if your neighbourhood is a little on the tidy side and lacking in nest-sites, put up several boxes close to one another.

House Sparrows also require insects in the breeding season to feed to their young, so make sure that you have a good selection of native and insect-friendly plants in the garden, too.

Finches

You don't have to look too far beyond seeds to keep finches happy in the garden. The type of seed favoured by each species is related to its bill shape as clearly as the pieces of a jigsaw puzzle fit together. And so, small seeds are eaten by those species with small bills, for example, and bigger, more unwieldy seeds by larger-billed finches.

Finches also vary in the way that they obtain their foods, from the ground, from herbs or from trees, or various combinations of the three, and they may be highly adapted to deal with just a few species of plant. This means that, to attract plenty of finch species to your garden, you need to plan well. It is also imperative for finches to have a ready water supply because eating seeds is a thirsty business and does not supply the birds with enough moisture to keep them going. The usual pond or bird bath will suffice, and these birds like it shallow.

A finch's bill is something pretty special – designed for the tricky process of de-husking

BELOW: *Now a rare visitor to most gardens, the Tree Sparrow will use nest-boxes if several are placed close together.*

ABOVE: *If you can bear it, leave a few thistles in for Goldfinches. Alternatively, provide nyjer seeds or sunflower hearts.* **OPPOSITE:** *Siskins usually visit in winter.*

seeds. When a bird is feeding, it lodges a seed in one of two grooves either side of the midline in the roof of its mouth. The seed now firmly held, the finch brings the sharp edge of its lower mandible (lower jaw) to bear upon it, cutting through the coating (husk). It then rotates the seed with its tongue and peels the husk off, exposing the kernel inside. The process described takes less than a second, but it explains why finches often seem to spend some time 'chewing' while they are on bird feeders.

The Goldfinch is a good example of a garden customer with quite specific tastes. It is a small, nimble bird, roughly the size of a Blue Tit, and its comparatively long bill is highly adapted for poking into tight spaces in order to obtain small seeds. It is actually a specialist at feeding from thistles, the seeds of which are in tightly packed heads, so the Goldfinch's bill works like a pair of tweezers to first force itself in and then pinch the seeds out.

Goldfinches are also the only birds that can manage to reach teasel seeds, perching on the spiky seed-heads like an entertainer lying on a bed of nails. In fact, tall herbs with tightly packed seed-heads, such as thistles, burdocks, sow-thistles, lavender and teasels, represent the unique niche of this species.

Most gardeners are wary of introducing thistles, although several types are available in garden centres if you do not mind a battle to control them. It is probably better – and somewhat more fashionable – to introduce teasel. This plant has the great benefit of remaining in situ even when the original stock of seeds has long gone. Then you can simply fill up the spent seed-head with niger and other favourites yourself. The birds will be delighted.

You don't necessarily have to bother growing specific plants to support Goldfinches, since they take with exceptional ease to hanging feeders, especially if small items such as nyger seeds are provided regularly. The problem is attracting the birds in the first place. You will have a head start in converting these acrobats to hanging feeders if you first attract them with tall herbs.

The Siskin is very closely related to the Goldfinch and has a similarly shaped, but slightly shorter, bill. It is equally adept at obtaining seeds from seed-heads that hang down and swing about, as thistles do for the Goldfinch, keeping hold with its strong feet; indeed, the Siskin prefers hanging upside-down when having a meal. At heart it is a lover of spruce seeds, especially in the breeding season, but in winter, when it is commonest in gardens, this passion turns to alder cones. If your garden soil is suitably moist you can in theory grow alder to attract it.

Such efforts, though, are not necessary to bring in Siskins. Since the 1960s, they have considered peanuts a perfectly suitable alternative and have followed garden feeding trends to black sunflower seeds, sunflower hearts and niger seeds, as if they had been reading the bird food suppliers' catalogues like us. All they require is a hanging feeder to dispense the food and their love affair with tree seeds will be forgotten.

The Greenfinch is a very different creature. It is a much larger, heavier bird than the Goldfinch or Siskin, and if it tried to emulate their tap-dance on the herb-heads it would probably fall flat on its face. It has a very broad bill that can deal with everything from tiny nettle seeds to old-fashioned striped sunflower seeds, but it needs a relatively sturdy perch to allow it a comfortable feed. It can perch on sunflowers to extract the seeds, but these are, of course, the helipads among flowerheads. In fact, the Greenfinch eats a great deal from the ground, and it can often be seen hoovering up spilt grain that has fallen from the bird table.

If the previous paragraph has made the Greenfinch seem a rather clumsy bird that is misleading – it is clumsy only in relation to the dainty Goldfinch or Siskin. As we have all seen, the Greenfinch is a regular visitor to most types of bird feeding station, and will cling vertically to mesh as well as using perches on hanging seed hoppers. It used to be a peanut fanatic, but the introduction of black sunflower seeds in the early 1990s changed its life forever. If given the choice, it will invariably opt for these, or, indeed, for sunflower hearts.

Greenfinches also eat certain foods that no other finch will touch. They are highly partial to yew berries, extracting the seeds and ignoring the pulp, and they also feed on rose hips (usually wild ones) and blackberries.

Unfortunately, these birds have the habit of taking possession of a perch or section of a bird feeder, remaining in place for minutes on end, while hungry birds have to wait. It is a bit like someone reading the newspaper in the toilet cubicle while a desperate

queue forms outside. The Greenfinch is not fussy, but it is fastidious, and will not be rushed.

The Chaffinch is a different kettle of fish from most other finches. Neither its bill nor its feet are particularly specialized, so it cannot easily take seeds except straight from the ground. It certainly cannot hold onto herbs like a Goldfinch, or to tree cones like a Siskin. It has a rapid pecking action that does not suit a struggle with a recalcitrant seed located in an awkward place. It can perch horizontally on seed-hoppers with adequate side perches, but in most gardens it is most at home below the feeders on the ground.

This finch feeds exclusively on insects in the summer, so it will benefit more than other finches from a garden policy of minimum chemicals and maximum native vegetation. It will breed where there is plentiful foliage, in thick shrubs or in trees.

Despite their reticent character, Bullfinches make a strong impact in the garden. It is not so much their beauty that strikes gardeners, as the shock of them munching large numbers of buds from a tender fruit tree or another choice plant, especially in early spring. Mild-mannered gardeners that help flies in spider's webs and make little homes for woodlice grow wild with anger when they see a Bullfinch working on their buds or blossoms, and they race out to chase it away. It seems to make it worse that the trespassing birds do not even look guilty, and feed with the same detached efficiency of a cow chewing the cud. When they are

ABOVE: *Old sunflower heads attract Greenfinches.*
BELOW LEFT: *Once a rare sight on the bird table, the Bullfinch has become an increasingly frequent visitor in recent years.* **OPPOSITE:** *Scenes from a bird-friendly garden. Tits crowd a hanging feeder, a Robin visits a nest-box, and a Great Spotted Woodpecker feeds alongside a Great Tit.*

really content and settled, the birds can devour 45 buds a minute, and strip a branch in one sitting – enough to make the nurseryman weep.

One positive way to protect your precious plants is to provide lots of food for the birds elsewhere. Bullfinches were once a very rare sight on bird tables or hanging feeders, but they are becoming more and more frequent in gardens, and some have even overcome their shyness to a degree. They come for conventional foods such as black sunflower seeds – and, to be honest, they would much rather be feeding on these than nutritionally impoverished soft parts of plants. The main reason that they come for buds in the first place is that there is a lack of available seed during this season. So put an extra feeder within sight of your buds, and both you and the Bullfinches should be able to live in harmony.

Chapter 6

Troubleshooting

The relationship between garden birds and bird gardeners is usually a smooth one, full of positives and pleasure. The birds get fed, the people get entertained, and only the bank balance of the latter suffers. However, into the mini Shangri La that we create there may well come a few unexpected problems, such as queue-jumping pigeons, voracious predators and junior victims of over-production. The fact that these unpleasantnesses take place in our personal idyll can make some among us disproportionally upset about them, but it's important as a bird gardener to keep a sense of balance. In this chapter we look at some of the more controversial issues surrounding birds and gardens.

ABOVE: *Juvenile Blue Tit: good Sparrowhawk food, or a victim?*
OPPOSITE: *Great Spotted Woodpecker on the look-out for trouble.*

Herons and Fish

People enjoy stocking their ponds with fish and herons, in turn, enjoy eating them. If you place fish in your pond you are simply filling a watery bird table, and the heron will gratefully accept your invitation unless discouraged.

Fortunately, if you are a gardener who loves birds and fish, but who wishes to stack the odds in favour of the latter, you can take a number of highly effective measures.

Try putting a tripwire around the edge so that the heron cannot wade in, or, if the problem persists, place netting over the water. A plastic or stone heron placed by the waterside will usually work, too, because herons are territorial and know that they are asking for trouble if they invade another heron's patch (rather like fishermen guarding their own spot). Make sure, though, that your model heron looks realistic!

And, if none of this works, buy cheaper fish.

BELOW: *To a Heron, a pond is just a watery bird table.* ABOVE RIGHT: *Love them or loathe them, Sparrowhawks are exciting birds to have in the garden.* OPPOSITE: *The problem of 'greedy' pigeons and doves is easily overcome.*

Sparrowhawks

People are usually delighted when they see their first Sparrowhawk in the garden. It is a moment when our beloved garden shows its wild, untamed face, and it can cause a frisson of delight. Over time, however, once the smaller birds on the feeders begin to succumb regularly, that delight can turn to concern, and even anger, and the thought arises that the slaughter must be stopped.

You have every right to feel what you feel, and if you really wish to prevent Sparrowhawks eating your other 'customers', then take the feeders down. Or you could site them under cover of branches, out of range of cats, which may impede the hawk's ambushes. But there isn't much else that you can do.

Never let yourself be tempted to think that the Sparrowhawk is taking 'too many' birds, and that in some way you have a duty to protect your smaller visitors. Quite aside from the fact that you probably cannot measure how many the hunter is catching anyway, this sort of thinking is dangerous and futile. The Sparrowhawk does eat plenty of birds, but it only kills for necessity and is utterly dependent on the food supply remaining buoyant.

In the ecological balance out there, Sparrowhawks simply won't reduce the numbers of songbirds to untenable levels because, if they did, they would do themselves out of their only food source. Put simply, if Sparrowhawks ate the smaller birds out of existence, they would starve.

Nobody denies that Sparrowhawks eat lots of birds, but, don't worry, a Sparrowhawk won't deplete your bird population to leave your garden quiet and soulless. On the contrary, a garden that is full of fit, predator-aware, resourceful birds, their survival skills honed by danger, will be a credit and a delight.

Too Many Pigeons?

As a birdwatcher and someone who is passionate about birds and natural history, I always find alarm bells ringing in my head when I hear the phrase: 'In my garden we have too many…'

The perceived culprits are often pigeons, which people tend to dislike rather than loathe, together with a number of other equally successful and unpopular species such as Magpies, Carrion Crows and Starlings.

What, exactly, does the phrase mean? What makes us deem a certain species to be a little more prevalent in our gardens than suits our taste? If you think about it, it is incomprehensible. We cannot deem a certain species' character particularly repellent because no bird is genuinely 'worse' than another. A species might act in a self-interested way that is harmful to another, but that's what birds do.

To take an example: people often abhor the killing of a Blue Tit by a Sparrowhawk, citing the former bird's relative defencelessness against the latter. But it should be remembered that Blue Tits in turn are merciless oppressors of Coal Tits, and while they don't kill them physically, they can rob them of their food and grind them down until they succumb due to lack of nutriment.

As for pigeons, they do indeed plonk themselves down on bird tables and prevent other birds feeding there, probably to the detriment of some smaller competitors. But they are no more 'greedy' than other species and should not be persecuted for that.

Happily, there are ways to deal with the problem, anyway. Pigeons like cereal grain and if you provide more specialized foods such as peanuts and sunflower seeds they will eventually express their disgust by trying their luck elsewhere. If you want to keep pigeons from a bird table or ground feeding station, that, too, can be achieved by acquiring 'cages' from bird food companies that have mesh of a size to let small birds in and keep larger birds out.

Gulls

The feathers of seaside suburbia have been ruffled in recent years by a proliferation of attacks by Herring Gulls. These are large, aggressive birds and what must be a reduction of their instinctive fear of humans has emboldened them to 'take us on', so to speak, in situations where previously they would have kept their distance. The result is that a certain number of people have had quite frightening experiences.

The most serious of these incidents have arisen in places where Herring Gulls nest on rooftops – a habit only acquired quite recently. Usually Herring Gulls breed in large colonies in flat places such as sand dunes and cliff-top turf, and because such sites are right out in the open, the birds are extremely highly strung and fierce in defence of their nest, eggs and young; in the face of attacks by foxes or people, you can begin to understand why. Naturally enough, rooftop gulls are no different, and they exhibit the same powerful urge to defend what is theirs.

The problem is that a Herring Gull territory has not just a horizontal component (their bit of roof) but a vertical component as well. Theoretically, not only is a section of roof 'theirs', but a part of

ABOVE RIGHT: *The Herring Gull (this is a 2nd winter plumaged bird) is a large, bold opportunist.*
BELOW: *'Who you lookin' at?'*

the loft, bedroom and lounge as well, at least in their eyes. An approach far below the actual nest is still an intrusion and a threat, and the birds respond in kind. This is why, when gulls breed so close to people, the occasional hapless pensioner feels afraid to go outside.

Magpies

Not long ago, a woman in Glasgow spoke on national radio about her war with Magpies. She boasted that she had killed over 100 of them in just a few months in her garden, and was pleased to report that the population of smaller birds in her area was increasing as a result.

You have only to look a little below the surface to see how her interpretation was flawed. For one thing, how did she know that the population of small birds was increasing at all? Had she counted or surveyed the relevant species? Of course she hadn't. Had she been able to prove a link between the perceived increase in small birds and a reduction in Magpie numbers? Hardly.

If she had really managed to kill 100 Magpies in the same place in a short time, was it not obvious that her local area had a large pool of recruits to fill the vacancies almost immediately, and therefore, that there would have been no effective diminution in active Magpies during that time to lead to the claimed increase in small birds? No. Naturally none of this had been considered, and it is sadly typical of the inaccurate, emotional and frankly prejudiced view that many garden bird enthusiasts have towards these black-and-white opportunists.

Now, if you hate Magpies just because you hate them, that's your privilege. If you hate Magpies because a pair raided several Blackbird nests last year and ate the young, that is also reasonable. But if you hate Magpies because you think they cause reductions in the numbers of small birds of your local area, you are on very shaky ground. Nobody denies that Magpies do raid nests and eat the eggs and young of some birds, and they cause much distress while doing so. But so far there seems to be little evidence that their worst efforts have much effect on the bird population in general.

Birds face a huge range of problems in their lives – starvation, disease, competition from their own and other species, disturbance, bad weather – and predation is just another of these. Most population declines can be traced to a variety of factors, and besides, breeding birds overproduce in order to cope with a dangerous world

Incidentally, Magpies very rarely kill any adult birds, so their presence in the garden simply does not 'keep the other garden birds away' as is often thought. Sparrowhawks are much more of a danger to adult birds, and their presence does not seem to stop the clientele visiting our bird feeders in their numbers.

In short, the 'problem' of Magpies in a garden is not as much of a problem as we might think.

ABOVE RIGHT: *One for sorrow...* **BELOW:** *The 'Magpie problem' is no black-and-white issue.*

Cats

Before you begin reading this section, please don't expect incendiary remarks about cat culls or other such things. Gardens and suburbia are habitats made by humans for human pleasure, and lots of people love cats, and wish to keep them. And so they should.

But cats don't half eat a lot of birds. They really are a major problem in the garden. They are far worse than Magpies, for two reasons: first, they take mainly adult birds, thereby striking at the breeding population; and second, they hunt birds throughout the year, whereas Magpies confine their miscreant activities to the breeding season only. If you would like to cull Magpies but own a cat, I for one would find it hard to respect your position.

It is estimated that between 25–70 million songbirds are killed by cats every year (the figure is disputed by the cat lobby, which is interesting psychology because, surely, the figure is not entirely relevant to the problem: how many dead birds are acceptable?) In an echo of the Magpie debate, it is hard to prove whether this toll has any effect in reducing the number of birds in gardens overall. Part of the problem is due to the fact that we have a large and poorly known population of gone-wild cats at large in our countryside, and

keep the moggies away. Planting thorny shrubs such as holly or gorse around bird feeding sites, or even surrounding your garden with them really can work. Putting nets over hedges to protect known nests is a good temporary measure, and you can site feeders away from cover where cats lurk. Always ensure that the predators can never reach the feeders by jumping or climbing. Finally, you can buy cat deterrent alarms that make an unpleasant ringing in the intruders' ears.

If you take all of these measures, you will have a very well-protected garden, and it will probably deter burglars, too! Mind you, the garden may look like a training ground for the SAS.

You could, of course, always buy a dog instead.

LEFT: *This feeder is temporarily closed.* **BELOW:** *Cats make wonderful pets, but collectively they do kill a lot of birds.* **OPPOSITE TOP:** *A Grey Squirrel raids a nest.* **OPPOSITE BOTTOM:** *All set to go!*

these take unknown numbers of birds, making the whole relationship hard to measure.

In the end, we know that cats and birds must coexist in gardens. Furthermore, there are several very positive measures that pet owners can take to make their animals less destructive to birds. A bell fitted to a cat will provide an early warning system of its approach, at least for a while. And if cats could be kept in at dusk and dawn, that would benefit the birds, too. It's not much to ask.

If you have a bird-friendly garden blighted by a high cat population, there are some things you can do to

Squirrels

I rather dislike Grey Squirrels but my kids love them, and that's the dilemma many garden owners face regarding these North American charmers. Some dedicated bird enthusiasts shoot them, but that is an extreme and not especially neighbourly thing to do. Others trap them and drown them or, probably worse, translocate them to sites where they will probably die, out of sight, through competition with the local squirrels. Other people encourage and feed them. They are tree-rats to some, Squirrel Nutkin to others.

Grey Squirrels are common nest predators, although the numbers of eggs and young they take may well not have any real effect on the population of birds in a garden, as is the case with Magpies. They are no easier to stop than the black-and-white birds, either. It's hard to see what you can do.

Squirrels also disturb the feathered visitors on bird tables and other feeders, gorging themselves on expensive food. This problem, though, is beginning to reduce now that you can buy squirrel-proof feeders of several kinds, most of which are highly effective.

Helping Baby Birds

We've all seen the sad results of some domestic mishap in the shape of helpless baby birds grounded in the garden, all alone and beseeching us for assistance. They might have fallen out of a nest, or apparently lost contact with their parent provider. It is very difficult not to have sympathy for them, and to want to intervene.

But just don't do it. Attempts to put a chick back in a nest, especially if it is feathered, can be catastrophic, because the remaining, relatively safe nestlings will greet your efforts by jumping out of the nest and scattering on the ground. It's an inbred escape response to extreme peril, and will leave you with several times the dilemma you started with.

To be honest, it's a good rule of thumb always to leave these chicks alone. If the adult is nearby and has not abandoned the youngster, as is usually the case, take yourself away – you are the problem. If the bird really has befallen calamity, its chances of survival are very slim. It's best to leave it and expunge your overdeveloped conscience.

Glossary

Advertising call: The equivalent of a song in a larger bird, such as a duck or gull.

Alarm call: A special call that birds give off only in situations of danger. The calls are often short and high pitched, so are difficult to locate.

Allopreening: The act of one bird, usually a pair member, preening the other.

Anvil: An object or surface used by a bird to break open items such as snails (Song Thrush) or seeds (Great Spotted Woodpecker)

Bounding flight: A more correct term for *Undulating flight* (see opposite).

Call: A sound, usually of short duration, made in reaction to some situation – e.g. alarm, maintaining contact with the rest of the flock etc.

Courtship-feeding: The act of a male bird bringing food to an adult female during the egg-laying and incubation periods, and sometimes beyond.

Crop: A large fold or extension of the gullet (oesophagus) used for storing food.

Crown: The top of the bird's head. (See *Bird Topography* opposite.)

Dispersal: A movement undertaken by juvenile birds once they have been evicted from their parents' territory, often taking them around the neighbourhood and beyond.

Display flight: A ritualised style of flying manoeuvre performed with or without a vocal accompaniment.

Dust-bathing: An unusual form of feather maintenance in which a bird literally spreads earth all over its plumage, probably to help remove parasites.

Egg-dumping: The act of a bird laying its own eggs in the nest of a neighbour of the same species.

Escape movement: A journey undertaken to evade a sudden, dangerous change in the weather.

Eye-ring: Refers to any distinctive colouration around the eye, shown on many birds.

Field mark: A distinctive plumage feature that makes a species recognisable from other similar birds.

First-winter: This refers to a bird that has hatched the previous spring and is therefore living its first winter of life. Also refers to the plumage worn at this time.

Flanks: The side of a bird that lies immediately under the folded wing. (See *Bird Topography* opposite.)

Fledgling: A young bird that has its first set of feathers and has left the nest.

Fly-over: Simply refers to a bird that has been seen flying over only (not landing).

Gamebird: A bird often shot for sport or food.

Immature: Any bird that is not yet in adult plumage (or, technically, not yet of breeding age).

Mandible: The name given to the upper and lower parts of the bill, equivalent to our upper and lower jaw.

Mantling: Refers to the practice of some birds of prey of spreading their wings over their prey to threaten any rivals and deter them from stealing the kill.

Moustache: A feature shown on the head of some birds. Usually a strip or bar running down the side of the cheek from the bill.

Nape: The back of a bird's neck.

Primaries: The largest flight feathers, making up the wing-tip. (See *Bird Topography* opposite.)

Rain-bathing: An unusual behaviour in which a bird exposes its plumage to the falling rain rather than taking a bath.

Rictal bristles: Small bristles around a bird's gape: they have a sensory function.

Rump: That part of a bird's upperside below the back and immediately above the tail. A rump is often brightly coloured and useful for identification.

Secondaries: See *Bird Topography* below.

Song: A series of sounds, often quite complex, made by a male songbird (in spring) to lay claim to a territory and/or attract a mate.

Song flight: A special ritualised style of flying or manoeuvre made for the specific purpose of accompanying a song.

Supercilium: Refers to a distinct line running over and past the eye, which is often called an eyebrow. Confusingly, and wrongly, it is called an eye-stripe in some books. The Redwing in the diagram below has a strong supercilium.

Territory: A patch of ground acquired, usually by a male bird, for the purpose of breeding (or sometimes feeding). Territories are exclusive and defended from other birds.

Tertials: See *Bird Topography* below.

Undulating flight: A flight course that takes a bird up and down rather than straight along at the same height. Many small birds do this.

Wing-bar: Much as it sounds, a more or less conspicuous stripe or bar along or across the wing.

Winter thrushes: Refers collectively to Fieldfare and Redwing, two species of thrush that are almost exclusively winter visitors to Britain.

Bird Topography

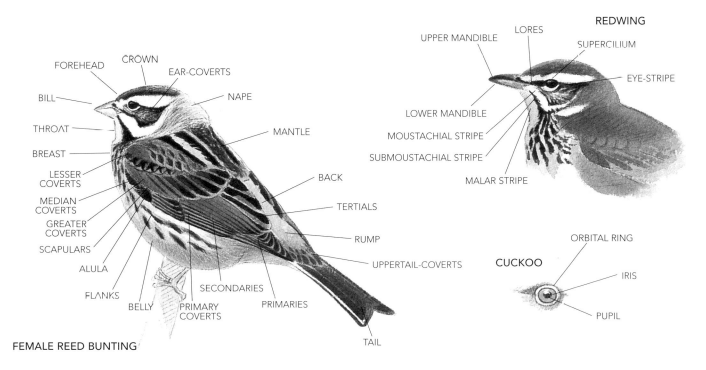

FEMALE REED BUNTING

FOREHEAD
CROWN
EAR-COVERTS
BILL
NAPE
THROAT
MANTLE
BREAST
LESSER COVERTS
BACK
MEDIAN COVERTS
TERTIALS
GREATER COVERTS
SCAPULARS
RUMP
ALULA
UPPERTAIL-COVERTS
FLANKS
SECONDARIES
BELLY
PRIMARIES
PRIMARY COVERTS
TAIL

REDWING
UPPER MANDIBLE
LORES
SUPERCILIUM
EYE-STRIPE
LOWER MANDIBLE
MOUSTACHIAL STRIPE
SUBMOUSTACHIAL STRIPE
MALAR STRIPE

CUCKOO
ORBITAL RING
IRIS
PUPIL

Useful Addresses

Birdlife International
Wellbrook Court
Girton Road, Cambridge CB3 0NA
Tel: 01223 277 318
www.birdlife.net

British Birdwatching Fair
British Birdwatching Fair Office
Fishponds Cottage
Hambleton Road, Oakham
Rutland LE15 8AB
Tel: 01572 771 079
www.birdfair.org.uk

BTO (British Trust for Ornithology)
The Nunnery, Thetford
Norfolk IP24 2PU
Tel: 01842 750 050
www.bto.org

C.J Wildbird Foods Ltd
The Rea Farm
Upton Magna, Shrewsbury
Shropshire SY4 4UR
Tel: 01743 709 545
www.birdfood.co.uk

Ernest Charles
Copplestone Mill
Copplestone, Crediton
Devon EX17 2YZ
0800 7316 770
www.ernest-charles.com

Garden Bird Supplies Ltd
Wem, Shrewsbury SY4 5BF
Tel: 01939 232 233
www.gardenbird.com

Jacobi Jayne & Co
Wealden Forest Park
Herne Common
Herne Bay, Kent CT6 7LQ
Tel: 01227 714 314

J E Haith Ltd,
65 Park Street
Cleethorpes
Lincolnshire DN35 7NF
Tel: 0800 298 7054
www.haiths.com

Rob Harvey Specialist Feeds
Kookaburra House
Gravel Hill Road
Holt Pound, Farnham
Surrey GU10 4LG
Tel: 01420 329 86
www.robharvey.com

RSPB (Royal Society for
the Protection of Birds)
The Lodge
Sandy
Bedfordshire SG19 2DL
Tel: 01767 680 551
www.rspb.org

The Wildlife Trusts
The Kiln
Waterside
Mather Road, Newark
Nottinghamshire
NG24 1WT
Tel: 0870 036 7711
www.wildlifetrusts.org

WWT (The Wildfowl &
Wetlands Trust)
Slimbridge
Gloucestershire GL2 7BT
Tel: 01453 891 900
www.wwt.org.uk

Books

*Bill Oddie's Introduction to
Birdwatching* (New Holland, 2002)

Birds by Behaviour, Dominic Couzens
(HarperCollins, 2003)

Birds of Europe, Lars Jonsson
(A&C Black, 1996)

Birdwatcher's Pocket Field Guide,
Mark Golley (New Holland, 2003)

Collins Bird Guide, Lars Svensson,
Peter Grant, Killian Mullarney
& Dan Zetterström
(HarperCollins, 2001)

How to Birdwatch, Stephen Moss
(New Holland, 2003)

*Pocket Guide to the Birds of Britain
and North-West Europe*,
Chris Kightley, Steve Madge and
Dave Nurney (Pica Press, 1998)

RSPB Handbook of British Birds,
Peter Holden and Tim Cleeves
(Helm, 2002)

The Secret Lives of Garden Birds,
Dominic Couzens (Helm, 2004)

Understanding Bird Behaviour,
Stephen Moss (New Holland, 2003)

Magazines and Journals

Bird Watching
Available monthly from newsagents,
or by subscription from Emap Active
Ltd, Bretton Court, Bretton,
Peterborough PE3 8DZ
Tel: 0845 601 1356

Birding World
Available by subscription from
Stonerunner
Coast Road, Cley next the Sea
Holt, Norfolk NR25 7RZ
Tel: 01263 741 139
www.birdingworld.freeserve.co.uk

Birdwatch
Available monthly from newsagents
or by subscription from Warners
West Street, Bourne
Lincolnshire PE10 9PH
Tel: 01778 392 027
www.birdwatch.co.uk

British Birds
Available by subscription from
The Banks, Mountfield Robertsbridge,
East Sussex TN32 5JY
Tel: 01580 882 039
www.britishbirds.co.uk

The Birdwatcher's Yearbook
Published annually by Buckingham
Press, 55 Thorpe Park Road
Peterborough PE3 6LJ
Tel: 01733 561 739
buck.press@btinternet.com

Index

Main references are denoted by **bold** pagination. Behaviour, plumage colours, calls and songs are indexed only where particularly distinctive.

Photography Acknowledgements

All photographs by Steve Young apart from:

Alan Williams: 18; 29; 112 bottom; 133.
George Reszeter: 17 top & bottom right; 76.
David Cottridge: 40; 82; 86; 109; 112 top; 138; 146.
David Tipling/Windrush Photos: 44; 110; 134.
Gordon Langsbury: 35.
Paul Sterry/Nature Photographers: 80
Ron Croucher/Nature Photographers: 169.
Tim Loseby/Windrush Photos: 135.

Artwork Acknowledgements

All artworks by Richard Allen apart from:

Dave Daly: 10; 12; 14 bottom; 16; 18; 21 top & bottom; 22; 23; 26; 28; 30; 32; 33; 34; 39; 40; 44; 46; 54; 57; 61; 63; 64 top & bottom; 65 top; 71 top; 78 top; 80; 81; 82; 83 bottom; 88; 92; 94; 95 top; 101; 109; 113; 116; 119 bottom; 125 top; 129; 130 top; 132 top & bottom; 138; 146 top; 147; 155; 167; 168; 171 left & right.